EFFECTIVE CLASSROOM MANAGEMENT

Effective Classroom Management

A Teacher's Guide

Robert Laslett and Colin Smith

CROOM HELM
London & Sydney

NICHOLS PUBLISHING COMPANY
New York

9401

© 1984 Robert Laslett and Colin J. Smith
Croom Helm Ltd, Provident House, Burrell Row,
Beckenham, Kent BR3 1AT
Croom Helm Australia Pty Ltd, First Floor,
139 King Street, Sydney, NSW 2001, Australia
Reprinted 1985

British Library Cataloguing in Publication Data

Laslett, Robert
    Effective classroom management.
    1. Classroom management
    I. Title II. Smith, Colin
    371.1'024   LB3013

    ISBN 0-7099-1627-2
    ISBN 0-7099-1628-0 Pbk

First published in the United States of America 1984 by
Nichols Publishing Company, Post Office Box 96,
New York, NY 10024

Library of Congress Cataloging in Publication Data

Laslett, Robert
    Effective classroom management.

    Includes index.
    1. Classroom management. I. Smith, Colin, 1938-   .
II. Title
LB3013.L37   1984   371.1'02   83-22080
ISBN 0-89397-177-4
ISBN 0-89397-178-2 Pbk

Printed and bound in Great Britain

CONTENTS

INTRODUCTION

We have written this book to help newly qualified teachers establish and improve their classroom management. In doing this, we realise that any authors who write about the management of children face difficulties, because they are not present in schools and classrooms where the significant events that affect management take place. We hope that we have reduced these difficulties facing us as far as it is possible to reduce them. We are experienced teachers, we are in contact with practising teachers, and we base many descriptive passages on observations in classrooms.

In our experience, it seems that effective teachers develop their own personal management practices without undue concern about the theories that underpin them. What we have tried to do here is to describe effective practice and also explain the theories that support it.

In some ways, effective classroom management is not unlike chess, although the comparison is not altogether satisfactory, because we do not regard teachers and the children in their classes as opponents. But it is true that experienced teachers know about opening moves and their effects on subsequent moves, they know which gambits are risky, and they know how to avoid checkmate and how to checkmate others. They also learn to study and respect the other person at the board. But even comprehensive knowledge of openings, middle and end games does not, of itself, ensure success. The knowledge has to be applied with sensitivity and imagination that can only come through practice. At the same time, this practice is improved by reading the accounts and confessions of successful chess players. Classroom practice is improved by studying what others do successfully and understanding the principles on which their practice is based.

We have written about management rather than control in classrooms, because we believe that management emphasises that learning and teaching are complementary activities. Just as successful managers in commerce and industry avoid disputes which disrupt production, so in the classroom successful teachers do not constantly have to demonstrate who is the boss. There are times when teachers must exert their authority clearly and unmistakably, and we do not pretend that it can be otherwise. But we also believe that good classroom management depends more upon teachers and children working equitably together because they are confident together, than upon peremptory instruction and resigned obedience.

1 FOUR RULES OF CLASSROOM MANAGEMENT

Successful classroom management has been defined as producing 'a high rate of work involvement with a low rate of deviancy in academic settings' (Kounin, 1970). Is there some special personal magic, which enables some teachers to quieten disturbance merely by arriving at the scene, quell misbehaviour with a glance, make classrooms bustle with activity and hum with cheerful industry? Perhaps, at that level of perfection, there is an extra ingredient, but studies of teacher behaviour have noted some specific skills which are demonstrated by successful teachers (Marland, 1975; Brophy and Evertson, 1976; Rutter *et al.*, 1979). Like the computations in arithmetic, these skills can be reduced to 'four rules', attention to which should enable all teachers to improve efficiency and harmony in their classrooms.

Rule One: Get Them In

The first rule requires attention to planning the start of each lesson. In a study of twelve London comprehensive schools, it was found that fewer behaviour problems arose where lessons started on time, and where teachers did not spend lesson time setting up or giving out materials. The process of beginning a lesson smoothly and promptly involves greeting, seating and starting.

Greeting

Simply by being present before the class arrives, the teacher establishes his role as host, receiving the class on his territory and, by implication, on his terms (Marland, 1975). Apart from the vital practical advantage of being able to check that the room is tidy, materials are available, displays are arranged and necessary instructions or examples are written on the blackboard, being there first allows the teacher to quietly underline his authority by deciding when the class comes into the room. In large schools, where various teachers share rooms, there may be difficulties, but professional commitment appears to be a more significant factor than distance between teaching areas (Rutter *et al.*, 1979).

1

Seating

Just how seating is arranged must depend on the type of lesson to be taught, and the type of classroom furniture. Whether using traditional serried ranks of desks or less formal group tables, each teacher needs to establish who sits where. Not only does this avoid an undignified scramble to sit nearest to or further from a particular child, the possession of a seating plan helps the teacher to learn names more rapidly (Marland, 1975). Later, it may be important to regroup children for some activities, to increase participation or decrease distraction, but initially at least a teacher should take quite arbitrary decisions, if necessary, to establish that placement and movement in his classroom are under his control (Francis, 1975).

Starting

Every lesson should start with some activity that keeps each child quietly occupied in his own place. What type of activity depends very much on the age and ability of the child and the nature of the lesson. Reading, writing, drawing or colouring may all be suitable in particular circumstances. What is most important is the need to give the children something which is clear and well within their capability. The aim at this stage is simply to buy a little time of peace and quiet to deal with latecomers, lost property or any other interruptions (Marland, 1975). Ideally, the work should involve reinforcement of previously acquired skills, particularly those required for the lesson which is about to be taught. Establishing a routine will require setting specific tasks and providing detailed verbal and written instruction. Having settled the class to work in this way, the temptation to leave them at it must be avoided. A few sums or a short paragraph to read with two or three questions to be answered should gain the four or five minutes which ought to be the maximum time for this opening activity; this can be seen as a period of warming up or tuning in, leading on to the main content of the lesson.

Rule Two: Get Them Out

However, before considering the content of the lesson, the second rule which needs to be mastered is how to conclude the lesson and dismiss the class. If this seems a strange order of priorities, it is worth remembering that if most disciplinary problems arise from a poor start to the lesson, hard-won control is most frequently lost and learning wasted at the end of lessons. The study of London comprehensive schools found that worse outcomes in terms of behaviour, academic attainment and attendance were found in schools where a greater proportion of lessons finished early (Rutter *et al.*, 1979). Planning the end of a lesson also seems to be part of the 'smooth transition from one activity to another' noted in an American study of successful teachers (Brophy and Evertson, 1976).

Concluding

Learning that has taken place during a lesson can often be wasted if an opportunity is not taken to reinforce what has been taught by a summary and brief question session. It is no use trying to do that over the heads of children who are still working or who are busy collecting exercise books. So at three minutes before the presumed end of the lesson, 'as precisely as that' (Marland, 1975), or at whatever time is judged necessary, work should stop, leaving an opportunity for the collection of materials, putting books away and some revision and recapitulation of the lesson.

If there is still time to spare, this can usefully be used for playing an appropriate game (see McNicholas and McEntee, 1973, for some examples of games that require no more than blackboard and chalk). It may well be that an established pattern, which involves an enjoyable game for all the class once desks are cleared, can be used as a reward for effort during the main body of the lesson, and an incentive for the prompt and orderly collection of materials at the end.

Dismissing

Once the bell does go, there is need for an established, orderly routine which ensures that the class gets beyond the door without the teacher having to spend time clearing debris from the floor or readjusting the lines of desks. If this can be done without recourse to sending out one section or row at a time, such informality is welcome. Traditional verbal prompting, 'arms folded, sitting up straight', may still have its place, however.

It is also important to remember that classes are never just leaving one place, they are going on to another. Children need to be cued in to their next activity. The following vignette is American, but its truth is universal.

Teacher It's time for PE now, everybody get ready. Table 1, line up at the door. Don't forget to pass your papers in. OK Table II, go ahead. Put your counting sticks away, everyone. Billy be quiet. Why aren't you cleaning up?

Students Ms Jones, we need our coats; it's cold out.

Teacher For goodness' sake, everybody sit down. You are much too noisy.

(Lemlech, 1979)

Here, because the teacher has not thought out the sequence for ending one activity and preparing for another, she has confused her pupils, and gone some way towards stimulating a quite unnecessary conflict over the children's behaviour. This teacher is displaying the tendency to 'flip flop' from one activity to another, then back to the first, which can cause momentum to drag during a lesson as well as disrupting its end (Kounin, 1970).

Rule Three: Get On With It

'It' refers to the lesson itself − its content, manner and organisation. Momentum is the key to determining the content of a lesson, its variety and pace.

Content

Variety is needed within a lesson to maintain interest, curiosity and motivation. Activities planned for the start and finish, as suggested above, will go some way towards achieving these aims. However, there is also a need to plan for some variety within the main body of the lesson. Two short lessons are likely to be more effective than one long one, and teachers should remember that a double period need not mean a double dose. Alternating preferred activities with more boring ones, mixing familiar work with new learning, and balancing quiet individual work with more active group tasks can all help keep a lesson moving (Sloane, 1976). It is essential, however, that variety should not become confusion. Each activity should be clearly specified and the teacher's expectations clarified so that each child knows what he should be doing and when he should be doing it. Just knowing what to do can remove the temptaton to misbehave. Giving precise instructions can be the simplest way to alter behaviour (Lovitt, 1977).

Pace is also helped by breaking up a topic into several smaller units of learning. It can also help to have as a target the intention that every child should have something finished, something marked in every lesson. Though often unattainable, such an aim does direct attention to the importance of immediate feedback and reinforcement in helping children to learn (Stott, 1978).

The momentum or flow of classroom industry is of great importance to discipline, as interruptions lead to loss of energy and interest on the part of pupils and teachers (Tanner, 1978; Rutter *et al.*, 1979). Although a general tendency to briskness appears desirable, the ability to vary pace, and to know when to teach less and allow more time for practice is also important. Short periods of practice followed by a rest or a different activity seem most effective (Lemlech, 1979).

Manner

Classroom atmosphere is a term frequently used, but rarely analysed. Here again, however, what might at first be thought to result from 'personality' can be described as a series of skills. Similarly, positive interaction between teacher and class can be traced to the way in which they communicate with each other. The skills involved in creating a good classroom atmosphere are really a series of mechanisms to regulate what goes on in the classroom.

'Withitness' was the now rather dated term used in one study to describe the teacher's ability to provide work at a suitable level and organise a system in which each pupil knew what he had to do, where to get help if he needed it, even if the teacher was busy, and what to do when he finished his assignment (Kounin, 1970).

In another study, teachers who 'monitored' class activity by frequently and vigilantly scanning the class, while moving around the room, helping individuals, made fewer 'target errors' (blaming the wrong child for a misdemeanour) and fewer 'timing errors' (waiting too long to intervene and precipitating distracting and disruptive confrontations) (Brophy and Evertson, 1976).

'Smoothness', an organised structured movement from one activity to another, is based on an almost automatic handling and, if possible, avoidance of problems through the use of student monitors, the provision of varied activities and plenty of materials (Brophy and Evertson, 1976).

Any system of class management needs some clearly defined rules, but these should be kept to a minimum. Observation has shown that in those classrooms with most frequent disciplinary interventions there is more disruptive behaviour (Rutter *et al.*, 1979). This may well result from the unofficial reinforcement gained from classmates for driving 'sir' or 'miss' to distraction. Teacher-baiting is one of the few blood sports still condoned in our society and some children are very good at it! It may be that frequent disciplinary interventions in themselves disrupt the smooth flow of activity and distract children from their work. Certainly, the more punishment dealt out, the more nagging that goes on, and the more negative the comments that are made, the more likely it is that tension will increase. Where intervention is necessary, it appears to be most effective where disruption is dealt with early, firmly and with minimum interference with the lesson in hand (Brophy and Evertson, 1976).

Behaviour does seem to be better and atmosphere brighter where ample praise is used in teaching (Hopkins and Conrad, 1976). Praise needs to be natural and sincere and should never become dull and routine. It is a good idea to try to think of at least six synonyms for 'good' and to use them appropriately. 'Great', 'superb', 'fine', 'splendid', 'remarkable' are some examples, or use more colloquial expressions such as 'ace', 'knockout' or 'cracker', if they come naturally. Similarly, 'nice' is a word so often used, when children would surely be more stimulated to know that their work was 'delightful', 'imaginative', 'beautiful', 'interesting', 'original' or 'fascinating'.

The way the teacher talks to the class reflects his attitude to them not only in what is said, but how it is said. Facial expression and tone of voice are as important to communication as making sure that attention is gained, by getting the class to stop work and listen carefully to what has to be said. It follows that what has to be said should be clear, simple and important enough to merit stopping the lesson.

The old adage, 'quiet teacher, quiet class' contains good advice, but should be followed with some reservation; 'inaudible teacher, insufferable class' may also be true. Adequate volume is an essential to being understood and it may help if teachers assume that in any class there is very likely to be at least one child with some hearing loss.

Emphasising the importance of using your eyes to communicate, what might be described as a 'lighthouse' technique is recommended by Marland (1975). Two or three sentences on a theme should be addressed to one child in one part of the room. As another idea is developed, the teacher shifts his gaze to another child in another part of the room, then focuses on a third for the next theme. This approach should help develop a 'feel' for what is going on in the different areas of the classroom. This is how to develop the traditional teacher's eyes in the back of the head. It also personalises communication, if remarks are addressed to people rather than the mid point of the back wall of the classroom. 'Look at them when you're talking to them', to adapt a certain comedian's catch phrase.

Another considerable part of classroom interaction involves the use of questions. Again, the teacher's attitude is reflected in the point and purpose of his use of questions. If these are seen as tricks and traps designed to catch out the unwary and inattentive, then they become a source of negative interaction. If the teacher sees questions as a way of checking whether his material is being understood, then a wrong answer can be seen as the teacher's fault, and the occasion for further explanation, rather than reprimand. Of course, this may not always be true, but as an orientation towards the purpose of questioning, it gives the teacher a far more positive perspective than the traditional assumption that wrong answers result from children's stupidity. A quiz can have its place, particularly as a way of recapping a lesson, but in the main body of the lesson teachers' questions should be a source of feedback rather than friction. If the lesson is to go smoothly, they should also be short, specific questions requiring brief answers and responded to with praise if possible, with tact if not.

Organisation

In any given subject, every class is a mixed-ability group. Whether dealing with high flyers or low achievers, teachers must allow for the fact that some children will work more rapidly and accurately than others. On the way to the ideal of individualising educational programmes for all their pupils, teachers can start by splitting their class into groups. The amount and difficulty of work demanded from each group can then be related to their abilities in that particular subject. There are three ways of doing this — by rota, quota or branching.

Rota, as in rotation of crops, refers to groups moving round the classroom from one activity to another. The development of learning centres is essential to this approach. These are areas of the classroom using alcoves, bookshelves or simply tables arranged to provide an environment for the accomplishment of a particular instructional purpose (Lemlech, 1979). They can be used for the practice of particular skills, gathering further information, extending experience or for instructional recreation.

Materials used to make centres might include books, worksheets, paper, pictures, magazines and tape cassettes. It is vital that access to the centres is controlled by the teacher and that there are clear instructions on purposeful activities for each centre. Rotation between the various centres is organised by the teacher, so that each group spends some part of each lesson, or a certain amount of time in each week, at the different centres.

An example adapted to a single theme might be for a remedial reading session to be divided between work: at a word-attack centre, where children complete worksheets teaching particular phonic skills; at a reading-with-understanding centre, where children answer comprehension exercises, work on cloze procedure or group prediction; at a games centre, where children play reading games. The amount of time spent at each centre, and the level of difficulty of the material encountered at each centre is determined by the teacher.

Quota similarly requires the teacher to work out an appropriate amount of work to be completed during a session by each group. Each child has an assignment card or booklet, which becomes a record of work completed as it is checked by the teacher. This system can be simply an extension of the rota system with individual requirements, such as reading to the teacher, handwriting or spelling practice being added.

Branching involves starting all the class together on a particular activity, doing an exercise from the board or working together from a textbook, then, as this is completed, 'branching' groups into different activities or areas of the room. For the quicker workers, who are likely to finish the common activity first, there may need to be a number of further pieces of work.

An example of this approach would be teaching a particular mathematical computation, showing examples and working through them on the board, then giving further examples to be worked from the board. As these are completed, more advanced problems or more concrete activities could be assigned according to results. Completion of the second batch of work could be followed by some recreational maths activity such as puzzles (Chester and Avis, 1977) or board games (Epps and Deans, 1972).

The branching approach lends itself more easily to traditional classroom arrangements, but can also be integrated with the use of learning centres. If centres are created, it is essential that a few simple rules are established to deal with 'traffic control' and 'noise abatement'. It is also vital that the activities provided should be stimulating and absorbing.

However attractive and well planned the content of a lesson, there remains a necessary element of goodwill on both sides to make it work. In this area, some understanding of child psychology, sympathy, understanding and, above all, a liking for children and a pleasure in their company will all help. Yet here again there are also observable teaching behaviours which can be practised.

Rule Four: Get On With Them

The temptation to misbehave is lessened where teachers and children get on well together. Many of the points already mentioned will help build a good pupil-teacher relationship, based on skilful, confident teaching geared to children's specific needs (Wallace and Kauffman, 1978). To further develop mutual trust and respect, the teacher also needs to show an awareness of each child as an individual and a sensitivity to the mood of the class as a whole. The teacher needs to know who's who and what's going on.

Who's Who?

Once a child's name is known, discipline is immediately easier, not only because the wrongdoer knows that he can be identified, but also because requests or rebukes can be made more personal; 'Quiet please, Quentin', 'Sit up straight, Cynthia' are preferable to remarks addressed to 'that boy at the back' or 'the girl over there'. Recognition also implies interest on the part of the teacher. It is easy to learn the names of the best and worst children, but less easy to remember those who do not attract attention to themselves. The attention is needed just as much, and sometimes more.

One useful way for teachers to check their awareness of individuals is to write down the names of all the children in the class without looking at the register. It may be interesting to note whether those hardest to bring to mind share any common characteristics such as shyness or average ability, undemanding of special attention (Lemlech, 1979).

There are other useful tactics to aid memory and increase awareness. A personal comment, using the child's name, can be written each time a book is marked. At least one question can be addressed to each child, every day, if not every lesson. A daily chat, however brief, about something not connected with lessons can be a source of insight as well as a way of establishing rapport. Best conducted through less formal contact in playtimes, dinner breaks and school clubs, it might be said that a chat a day, keeps trouble at bay! As with praise, personal interest must be natural and genuine, not merely assumed.

What's Going on?

Few classes of children are likely to be so purposefully malevolent as to set out on a planned campaign of disruption. Group misbehaviour is more likely to build up from a series of minor incidents. It is necessary therefore for teachers to acquire a sensitivity to group responses. The key to developing this talent lies in a combination of monitoring, marking and mobility (Brophy and Evertson, 1976).

Frequently scanning the class, even while helping one individual, should enable the teacher to spot the first signs of trouble quickly and intervene firmly but quietly. Often, merely moving to the area from which the shuffling feet or louder voices are indicating some distraction can refocus attention on the work in hand. The mild personal rebuke addressed to an individual at his desk can be far more productive than a formal public warning.

Marking work in progress is not only a good way of giving immediate feedback, it is also a natural form of contact. Rather than reprimanding the child who is not concentrating on his work, offering help and advice may be the best way to return his attention to the task in hand. Good marking implies careful record keeping, not only in the sense of formal documentation, but also in the form of easy access to the knowledge of what each child has done, what he should have done and what he is going to do next (Marland, 1975).

Mobility is needed to avoid teachers becoming desk-bound by queues waiting for attention, which can screen inactiviy elsewhere in the classroom and themselves become social gatherings and a potential source of noise and distraction. It is essential to develop a routine, which enables children to find help from each other if the teacher is occupied, or which provides them with alternative purposeful activities while waiting for advice or correction. This will free the teacher to move around the room, sharing his time and interest, adding all the time to his awareness of personalities and problems.

It is this combination of activities that enables the responsive teacher to judge correctly the times for serious endeavour or light-hearted amusement.

Teacher Credibility

These four rules of class management are no panacea for trouble-free teaching. They might be seen as a checklist for the assessment of what has been neatly described as 'teacher credibility' (House and Lapan, 1978). Attention to these four areas will not solve all the problems of disturbed, disruptive and disaffected pupils, but it should avoid problems caused by disorganised teaching.

2 MAINTAINING A PEACEFUL CLASSROOM ATMOSPHERE

In any lesson there is some potential for pupil disruption. In recent years, the growth of mixed-ability teaching, often necessitating group work, has increased that potential. Teachers today are therefore more vulnerable to time-honoured ploys, which children have always used to gain distraction from their work. The four main sources of friction are characterised by Francis (1975) as noise, equipment, movement and chatter. None in itself is a major challenge to the teacher's authority, but each, if wrongly handled, can develop from a minor irritation into a major confrontation.

Minor Irritations

Noise might, for example, involve shuffling feet or papers, shifting of desks or scraping of chairs, unnecessary coughing or, in one of the worst manifestations, what might be described as wilful flatulence! Even attempting definition indicates how petty the offence is and how difficult it is to frame an accusation concerning it.

Equipment loss or induced malfunction is another potent source of disruption, particularly with the excellent opportunities provided for the display of injured and exaggerated innocence. Protests that 'I did have a ruler, but someone's taken it' or 'I can't help it, if the pencil keeps breaking' can be especially irritating, if the teacher feels the class share his suspicion that this is a contrived event.

Movement is inevitably more of a problem now than in the days of static sessions of 'chalk and talk'. With more fluid group activities, there is a temptation to wander off for a gossip and a giggle. When apprehended, patently false claims to have been in search of material or pretended fascination with the work of another group add to the teacher's sense of being subtly provoked.

Chatter, too, presents more possibilities for dispute in an educational setting which encourages children to comment on their work, than in an era where talking except in answer to a teacher's question was simply prohibited. Once the pupils' right to discuss together the work in hand is conceded, even encouraged, then the volume and relevance of what is said can easily become matters of contention.

Having used such ploys themselves quite recently, young teachers are prone to over-react. Sensitive to the challenge which is there, albeit minimally at first, fearful that they will be thought an easy mark, if they do not take up the challenge, and mindful of their own opinion of 'weak' teachers, they often respond with dramatic and would-be draconian harshness, which is counter-productive.

Some of these problems can be avoided by giving careful thought to the assignment of responsibilities for the distribution and collection of equipment. Marland (1975) suggests keeping a note on the blackboard of items such as brushes or scissors given to particular groups, with the name of the person responsible alongside. Similarly, rules can be established to regulate movement and chatter by limiting walking and talking to particular parts of the room. Establishing a few essential rules and clarifying what is acceptable conduct is often sufficient to avoid problems arising, for, as Lovitt (1977) points out, most children 'if they know what we want them to do, will do it'.

Such precautions will not prevent the calculated provocation or deliberate affront, although they will deter the casual transgressor. Even when quite certain that misbehaviour is intentional and provocative, the teacher must beware of too strong an immediate response. Anger, even if simulated, uses up too much adrenalin and using heavy punishments for minor infractions leaves nothing in reserve for more serious cases. Rather, the teacher should look for a series of responses which are cool, calm and carefully calculated.

Appropriate Responses

Although derived from their treatment of maladjusted boys over thirty years ago, Redl and Wineman's (1952) amusing description of 'techniques for the manipulation of surface behaviour' still provides a useful framework for discussing appropriate responses to milder manifestations of misbehaviour.

At this stage, misbehaviour is most likely to result from seeking attention, escaping from boredom or warding off inadequacy. It should not be seen as a battle for power or an attempt to gain revenge, although these motives may soon become involved if the situation is mishandled. With tongue fairly evidently in cheek, Redl and Wineman use some amusing bits of pretentious-sounding jargon to describe how teachers handle problems which are 'on the surface', rather than deep rooted.

'Planned Ignoring'

Some provocative behaviour will rapidly exhaust itself unless attended to by the teacher. As noted above, it is often difficult anyway for the teacher to attend to some misbehaviour without sounding foolish. Indefinite noises, muttered imprecations and parroting instructions are examples of actions best met initially by selective deafness or blithe indifference.

However, the emphasis must be on *planned* ignoring, rather than just hoping the nuisance will go away. Deafness, for example, must be credible in the circumstances or it will merely embolden louder attempts to provoke a reaction. Pretended lack of awareness of the undesirable behaviour should be linked to positive attention to the work in hand.

'Signal Interference'

If apparent ignorance is not working, the next stage requires an attempt to inhibit the unacceptable behaviour by making it clear that its source has been spotted. This signal should block further malpractice, rather as one radio station might jam another by providing 'interference'.

Once eye contact has been made, teacher's signals may take the form of gestures such as using a frown, raised eyebrows, a shake of the head, or a wave of an admonishing forefinger. Often the signal may involve a quiet, personally addressed request to desist. What is most important is ensuring that the signal is received. As Long and Newman (1976) point out, some children would have you stand and look at them all day without it helping control their behaviour one bit.

It is also vital to see that the signal is not perceived as a distress signal! The apparent success of verbal criticism and prohibition can easily lead teachers into the trap of believing that nagging works. As quiet admonitions become louder reprimands, teachers can rapidly find themselves at the yelling stage (Poteet, 1973). Once at this point, control and dignity are easily lost. Teacher-baiting is probably the only blood sport widely accepted in modern society, and once the scent of hysteria is caught the most placid and well-intentioned children will join the hunt!

Proximity Control

If a signal has failed, restlessness and excitement may be calmed by the physical proximity of the teacher. Just by being close at hand, the teacher can provide a source of protection and orientation. Most children will stop irrelevant activity and chatter and resume their work once a teacher is near. If they do not, then a more serious problem presents itself!

To be successful, 'proximity control' needs to be tried at an early stage, before misbehaviour has got very far. It also needs to be associated with 'interest boosting'.

Interest Boosting

The teacher's attention and display of interest in a child's work can refocus attention. Intervention should be specific, rather than general. For example, 'Have you remembered to pay back?' rather than: 'How are you getting on with those sums?'

Marking work done so far is an easy way to intervene, offering help with the task, rather than confrontation over behaviour. This implies an assumption, which is often true, that distraction has resulted from inability to cope with required work.

Marking may give an opportunity to praise and remotivate: 'All correct so far' or 'That's an interesting start to your story'. It may be necesssary to demonstrate, especially if little work has actually been done. 'Let me show you again how to set these sums out. I'll put them in your book, then you fill in the answers.' This gives the teacher a chance to modify the difficulty of the task.

Sometimes an alternative activity can be suggested: 'Leave that question for now. Trace the map instead.' Obviously the alternatives should be relevant to the topic being taught, and the difficult task is deferred, not avoided. Otherwise the pupil merely learns another useful work-avoidance technique and sees the alternative activity as a reward for messing about.

Hurdle Help

With many children 'interest boosting' will merge with the technique described as 'hurdle help'. For some pupils, particular lessons will present immediate problems, or hurdles, which they cannot surmount without asistance. Unless helped, these children will rapidly become frustrated and fractious. Once aware of their problems, the teacher can make sure that they get early individual attention when approaching an area of difficulty.

Some children may need help in reading through a problem, some need more help with spelling, others will need reminding about how to set out their work. The teacher's tactic should be to provide some assistance, not to collude at avoidance. Initially, it may be appropriate to do some of the work for the child who is floundering, but the aim is not to remove the hurdle so much as give a push to help him over it. Thus the child with a particular problem with spelling can be helped with key words, but also encouraged to use a dictionary.

Goals of Misbehaviour

Used together, the techniques of proximity control, interest boosting and hurdle help should cope with the type of misbehaviour which develops as a means of warding off inadequacy. However, this is only one of the possible goals of misbehaviour described by Dreikurs, Grunwald and Pepper (1971). The child who is not getting on with his work might also be seeking attention, revenge or power; Charles and Malian (1980) suggest that misbehaviour directed towards 'getting even' or establishing control is likely to take the form of making a deliberate mess, destruction of work, stealing, viciousness, lying or blatant disobedience. It is unlikely that the minor transgressions described so far would be motivated by the desire for revenge or power.

If there is a resentful sullen response to offers of help or if the pupil fiercely argues back when offered advice, then more serious problems may be inferred. None the less, the teacher's initial assumption that difficulties concern work rather than personal animosity may in itself divert all but the most determined seekers after confrontation.

Attention seeking is the far more probable intention of most minor misdemeanours. As with inadequacy, if the teacher's attention is given to the task rather than the behaviour, there is an opportunity to avoid conflict.

Often pupils themselves are unaware of the goals of their misbehaviour and revealing the intents and purposes of their actions may eventually be beneficial (Egan, 1981). Instant and public attempts at psychotherapy, however, are unlikely to have advantageous results. Discussion of motivation is more likely to be seen as a challenge to the child's capacity for provocative wit or studied indifference.

Concentration on what the pupil is doing, rather than why he is doing it, can often defuse a potentially tense situation. If this does not work, Redl and Wineman have some further techniques for at least temporarily influencing 'surface behaviour'.

Tension Decontamination Through Humour

When there is a confrontation between teacher and pupil, it is as if the classroom atmosphere becomes contaminated by the invisible posioned gas given off by anger and tension. The air can be cleared by a well-timed joke or comment which draws attention to the funny side of the situation.

Such responses are spontaneous by their very nature and cannot be planned. Humour differs from place to place and time to time. What one group of children might consider a sharply amusing aside, another might find hurtful and sarcastic. Perhaps the essential feature is the ability of teachers not to take themselves too seriously. Long and Newman illustrate this technique by quoting a teacher who upon discovering an unflattering portrait on the blackboard, comments on the good likeness, but adds 'you forgot my glasses' and, picking up the chalk, proceeds to draw them.

Hypodermic Affection

Coping with anxiety and frustration can be helped by an 'injection' of praise or affection. The teacher needs to make sure that the needle with which this injection is adminstered is not a blunt one. In other words, for this technique to work it is essential that the praise is valued and the affection is appreciated. With some children, being singled out for praise in front of their friends can have a negative rather than a positive effect. Affection, too, can be a problematic concept. What is intended here is the need to convey a genuine liking rather than a cloying senti-mentality. In a classroom where praise is frequent and the teacher's enjoyment of the company of children is evident, then an extra dose will not come amiss.

Direct Appeal

Sometimes developing trouble can be averted by the teacher making a direct appeal to the pupil's sense of values. Although it would be cynical to suggest that children today lack a sense of co-operation, fair play and kindness, these values are least likely to be held in high esteem by the sort of pupil to whom it may be necessary to address a direct appeal to stop misbehaving. It might also be argued that where such values are present, they are least likely to be displayed in a group: witness changing football-crowd behaviour in the last twenty years!

Whether appealing to the individual or the class, the value areas more likely to be responsive to appeal concern a sense of reality, possible consequences and self-preservation. Thus appeals might be made in terms of authority. For example, 'I can't allow you to do that', or of peer reaction: 'If you talk, the others can't hear the story'. As with the most traditional appeal to pupil realism, 'If you don't do it now, we'll do it at playtime', there is a fine line between appeal and threat, and the distinction needs to be clear in the teacher's own mind before he can expect the pupils to understand it.

The most effective appeal is the personal one made on the basis of a good relationship: 'Do you really think I'm being unfair?' As with injections of praise and affection, direct appeal is a technique best deployed only after getting to know children very well indeed. As Egan states, it requires 'a great deal of practice and teachers' "savvy"'.

The preferred course of action remains the avoidance of tension or disruption. Rather than the intervention at the individual level suggested by the last half-dozen techniques, it is often appropriate to rely on organisational or group management techniques.

Support from Routine

Settled patterns of organisation help pupils and teachers know where they stand and what to expect. Weber (1982) shows the way in which the flow and movement of the typical secondary-school timetable can disturb and confuse slow learners. As the day goes on, successive teachers using different approaches present classes with varied and sometimes conflicting views of how they are expected to behave. He quotes an example of one school where problems with a particular class were solved by the staff reaching an agreement on a common policy for lesson organisation.

All teachers started work with a short exercise from the board, so that pupils got into the habit of entering each class, going to their seats and starting work straight away. Similar practices were adopted in other parts of structuring the lesson. As Weber points out, this did not need to be a rigid, inflexible routine leading to impersonal uniformity. Teachers could still express their individuality in the way they presented the content of the lesson, but, by adopting a shared policy towards management, they avoided the confusion that can arise from varied expectations. Pupils knew that whoever was teaching them, certain behaviours were encouraged and others were not acceptable.

A predictable pattern of activities within the lesson also helps maintain a comfortable, stable atmosphere. It provides 'markers' for pupils and teachers, which help pace the rhythm of the lesson, easing transition from one activity to another.

Actual routines will differ according to subjects to be taught, but the basic plan is usually the same.

Start with seatwork, recapping work previously taught.
Introduce new work through teacher talk or demonstration.
Make sure pupils grasp the new ideas by question and answer session.
Practice examples by working as a group and then individually.
Look back by reviewing the new learning and linking it to previous skills and knowledge.
Enjoy a game, story or some other form of relaxation.

Those readers who like mnemomic acronyms will notice that this plan is SIMPLE. Readers who do not like mnemonic acronyms might like to find an alternative plan of their own, but it will still need to be simple. Once routines become overelaborate, teachers and pupils tend to lose their place.

Restructuring

There are occasions when the best-planned lessons can begin to go wrong. Excitement, noise or disruptive action can build up to such an intensity that teachers feel the need to change to a different quieter activity.

Routine can help here, too. If the excitement starts to become hysterical during the introductory demonstration phase, then the teacher can move more rapidly than originally intended to the pupil-centred practice activity. Thus a worksheet planned to follow a discussion may be brought out earlier to replace discussion, if the class is too noisy or distractable to concentrate.

Sometimes material proves more difficult than teachers expect. Sometimes individuals seem intent on disrupting loosely structured activities. Sometimes a whole class, or most of it, will have an off day when communal silliness breaks out. (Without backing from any known research, many teachers assert that this usually happens around the time of the full moon!) Whatever the reason, teachers do often need to resort to the technique Redl and Wineman refer to as 'restructuring'.

The danger with this approach is the tendency for teachers to threaten children with practice exercises like sums or worksheets, when these are intended to be pleasurable and intrinsically motivating experiences. Also, the children who are least able to handle the comparative freedom of discussion or experiment are quite likely to prefer the regulated familiarity of mechanical arithmetic.

More usefully, this technique is employed in bringing forward more easily managed parts of the lesson, without, as it were, admitting defeat. The teacher implies that, even if incomplete or unsuccessful, the work done is not totally unsatisfactory. For example, 'We'll discuss this topic again another day, but now I want you to do some written work'. 'I think we'll stop there for today. When the materials are all collected, I want to get on to the next chapter in our story.'

The teacher is indicating that he is still in charge of the situation. He is not shocked, disturbed or overcome by the way matters have developed. Remonstration only leaves some pupils feeling guilty that they have let their teacher down, while others feel a glow of victory at upsetting him.

Self-evaluation

Other techniques described by Redl and Wineman include removing distracting objects during lesson time, the application of physical restraint and the brisk removal or 'antiseptic bouncing' of disruptive pupils. These measures relate to conflict and confrontation, rather than the theme of this chapter, which has been concerned with preventing mild misbehaviours from becoming more serious matters of contention between teacher and pupil.

The responses which have been suggested need to be applied flexibly and with frequent self-evaluation. The teacher should relate them to questions about the content and manner of teaching.

Content

Smith (1979) suggests that looking back on lessons teachers should ask themselves:

'What worked today and what didn't?'
'Was the work too hard or too easy?'

'Was there enough variety and change of pace?'
'Were there enough alternatives to fall back on?'
'Was there enough revision? Did I repeat, rephrase, refresh, restate the concepts, vocabulary and information?'
'Did I ask the right kind of questions?'

Manner

'Did I give enough attention to positive behaviour?'
'Did I give too much attention to negative behaviour?'
'Did I ignore too much or too little?'
'Did I fuss or nag too much?'
'Did I praise sufficiently?'
'Was there enough humour in the lesson?'

Answers to these questions will help teachers pitch lessons at the right level of difficulty and preserve a pleasant and peaceful classroom atmosphere.

3 EXPECTATIONS AND ORGANISATION

Teachers' expectations are based on knowledge of pupils' past performances and perceptions of their present ability, motivation and behaviour. Conveyed to pupils in a variety of subtle ways, these expectations can have a powerful influence in helping or hindering the development of a child's image of himself as a competent learner (Brophy and Good, 1974). Although personality factors are also involved, expectations are shaped and changed mainly by contacts concerned with task activities. Lesson organisation can therefore make a major contribution to the promotion of cordial relationships and positive attitudes.

Generalising from a number of correlational studies, Brophy (1979) claims that successful teaching, as measured by class learning gains, is linked to certain patterns of teaching behaviour, rather than specific personal characteristics or disciplinary methods. These patterns are described in terms of firm commitment to an instructional role and confidence in the teacher's ability to get pupils to learn. Effective teachers know how to organise their classroom to 'maximise time on productive activities' and minimise time lost on transitions, periods of confusion and disruptions. This view echoes the findings of Rutter *et al.* (1979) and is further supported by Evertson (1982), who also concurs with Brophy's suggestion that lower-ability groups particularly benefit from direct instruction in a clearly structured curriculum. Thus organisation can be seen not only as an essential teaching skill, but also as the means by which a teacher can demonstrate positive expectations.

Individual Expectations

Differential expectations are shown by the way teachers talk to different children, by the way they ask them questions and by the amount of time they spend with them. Looks, stance and posture are other nonverbal indications of teacher attitude which can convey to pupils that, although some 'are bright, capable and responsible, others are dull, incapable and irresponsible' (Jones and Jones, 1981).

Teachers behave differently towards groups of whom they have high expectancies than towards those from whom they expect little. In a celebrated experiment (Rosenthal and Jacobson, 1968), teachers were told that certain pupils had shown by their performance on a new psychological test that they were about to make dramatic progress. In fact these children had been chosen at random, but nevertheless, at the end of the year, the experimental group had improved their perform-ance on tests of general abilities and reading achievement by more than their classmates. It has proved difficult to replicate this demon-stration that elevated teacher expectations can become self-fulfilling prophecies (Rutter and Madge, 1977). Perhaps the wide publicity and exaggerated claims for the original experiment made teachers beware of psychologists bearing 'gifted' children? In an extensive review of rele-vant research, Brophy and Good (1974) dismiss the over-simplification that high expectation on its own can become almost magically self-fulfilling. They advance a more subtle view of the way in which observation and inference, based on a pupil's performance, interact with a teacher's feelings and reactions towards a pupil's personality.

Differential expectations are inevitable. It is not possible or desirable to expect the same performance from all pupils, nor is it possible to treat them all exactly the same way, because they all have different abilities and individual needs. What matters most is the teacher's aware-ness of his expectations and flexibility in his approach. In their own study, Brophy and Good (1974) noted three ways in which teachers responded to pupils for whom they had high or low expectations.

Over-reactive teachers have rigid and stereotyped perceptions, dis-missing the 'slow learner's' capacity to improve or the 'troublemaker's' potential for reform. They therefore tend to underestimate what some children can do and give up easily with poor performers.

Reactive teachers are less likely to exacerbate perceived differences by an inflexible approach. However, they tend to be passive in their acceptance of low achievers, rather than active in trying to compensate for differences.

Proactive teachers are more ready to take the initiative in over-coming learning problems. Realistic perception of difficulties will be used to plan individual instruction, and interventions will be made to preserve a balanced participation in class activities for high and low achievers.

The first two types are likely to spend more time working with high achievers, allowing, or in some cases encouraging, the brighter, hard-working children to dominate classroom activity or discussion. Whether through rejection in the case of over-reactors or neglect by reactive teachers, the low achiever receives less attention. In turn, he reacts by either passive acceptance of his own limited potential or over-reacts by extreme behaviour and a stereotyped rejection of teachers and teaching. There are no studies of proactive low achievers. Although some children will try to compensate for lack of interest by trying harder, it should not be surprising that they give up more easily than adults!

Another group of teachers described by Brophy and Good (1974) might be called 'overcompensators'. Although they are aware of the problems of less able children and anxious to accommodate them, these teachers adopt strategies which, though overtly sympathetic, may inadvertently aggravate the situation.

Inappropriate behaviours on the part of the teacher, which, however well-intentioned, consistently emphasise the inadequacy of a child, can sharpen the other children's awareness of differences. Being picked out for special treatment can easily become, for the child concerned, an experience of being picked on for special embarrassment. Some examples of such inappropriate behaviours would be giving markedly more time for answers to relatively simple questions. Fulsome praise for patently inadequate work or persistent and publicised setting of easier tasks are other examples of the debilitating effects of special attention.

Additional support for the slow learner should be as unobtrusive as possible. Though expectation of intellectual attainment may be different, socially the teacher should treat the slow learner as one of the group, emphasising similarity rather than difference. This process will be helped if, within the class, progress is related to individual rather than comparative performance — each child competing against his own previous best effort, rather than trying to beat other children.

Class Expectations

As well as differential expectations for individual pupils, teachers also vary in their expectations of success or failure with classes in general (Brophy and Evertson, 1976). Just as the individual gathers an impression of his teacher's expectations from a number of subtle and not so subtle signals, so a class quickly gathers a collective impression of the teacher's reaction to them.

Henson and Higgins (1978) suggest that 'personalised' teaching is the most effective way to stimulate intrinsic motivation and promote group enthusiasm for learning. In their view, the teacher should provide a good 'model' for class behaviour by showing interest in each member of the group, by knowing names and treating with courtesy; by showing patience in recognising academic limitations and setting work accordingly; and by showing fairness in balancing shares of time and attention. This individualised approach is projected within a classroom 'humanised' by having only a few simple and essential rules, and by the teacher's avoidance of threats, public reprimands or ridicule. Lessons should contain challenge by presenting contradictions to be resolved, but not problems so difficult that pupils give up. Although lessons should be as informal as possible, the teacher should provide structure and display enthusiasm through excitement, intonation and humour.

Johnson and Johnson (1975) also see the teacher as a facilitator promoting a comfortable atmosphere, easing communication and establishing trust. The teacher's effectiveness in their view depends on his competence in setting suitable goals, assembling resources and materials, providing constructive advice and letting pupils know how they are getting on. They strongly urge the value of getting groups of children to work together towards a common goal, emphasising co-operative rather than competitive or individualised learning.

Though also concerned with the need to convey enthusiasm, Robertson (1981) devotes considerable attention to the teacher's need to 'communicate authority'. Status and dominance can be conveyed by posture, maintained eye contact and use of territory. Thus the teacher establishes his dominant position by expecting an upright and attentive posture from his pupils, 'staring down' any challenging gaze and making clear that, although certain behaviour is required at the teacher's desk, the pupil's own desk or personal space can be entered by the teacher in a direct and immediate way; for example, to remove a distracting object. Authority is also communicated by the manner in which the teacher addresses the class, establishes silence and administers reprimands.

These three studies illustrate different teaching styles, but in each case, whether as personaliser, faciliator or authority figure, the teacher is intent on creating an impression as someone who treats the class in a particular way. The choice of teaching style may often depend on the age-group to be taught. Henson and Higgins are writing about working in junior schools, Robertson is more concerned with helping young teachers deal with senior pupils, and Johnson and Johnson's approach has perhaps most relevance to the middle years. The common feature of all three prescriptions is the manner in which the teacher's expectations are made explicit and children are therefore able to predict the type of response expected from them.

Good and Brophy (1980) strongly urge the importance of project-ing positive expectations both for attainment and conduct as a way of enhancing the pupil's self-image;

> Students treated as basically good people who want to do the right thing, whose lapses are treated as due to ignorance or forgetfulness are likely to become the prosocial people they are expected to become. Students treated as if they are inherently evil or under the control of of powerful antisocial impulses, whose lapses are taken as evidence of immorality rather than as isolated mistakes, probably will turn out to be antisocial, just as expected.

Considerate Organisation

Sometimes the conditions and consequences of learning appear to be arranged in ways which discourage all but the most competent of pupils. There are a number of aspects of lesson planning and presenta-tion which together make up what has been described as the 'class-room environment' (Martin and Lauridsen, 1974). These can be examined by asking a number of questions, the responses to which show that positive expectations can be demonstrated by considerate organisation as well as personal treatment.

Subject Matter

Is a subject area one on which the pupil has previously failed? Is this failure reinforced by the pupil's own awareness of his low achievement? If incompetence has been stressed in the past, certain subjects are approached in such a defeatist manner that children are ready to give up before they even start.

It is not enough for teachers to remain doggedly cheerful in the face of ignorance and incomprehension. Though preferable to irritation and scorn, sympathy too can sometimes add to a sense of humiliation. The teacher needs to convey a belief that this time the child really can succeed. This belief should be based on a genuine effort to reorganise, restructure and redesign material so that, although content and skills to be mastered remain the same, the experience of learning them is changed. Just as a failed commercial product is often successfully repack-aged and relaunched, so teachers need constantly to resell subject areas. Even if previous failure has produced a thorough dislike of a subject as a whole, a fresh approach can stimulate interest in a particular topic or get children to tackle specific skills with a new vigour. One simple example is the way in which even older slow learners who would baulk at yet another attempt to learn number bonds or multiplication tables will readily tackle the same calculations disguised as algebraic equations.

Presentation

Is material presented in a manner which captures the pupil's interest? Do pupils get bored easily? Do they respond better to certain parts of the lesson? Although a predictable pattern to lessons provides 'support from routine', this does not mean that curriculum materials and presentational formats should remain unchanged. The unremitting plod through a standard textbook can be the most dispiriting part of failure in a particular subject. In planning to avoid this, ingenuity is needed to provide a variety of lesson content. Film, television, radio and tape recording can all be useful, and computers are becoming an increasingly familiar teaching aid, offering a particularly attractive method of taking the drudgery out of drill and practice.

Variety can also be achieved by arranging a mixture of oral and written work, individual and group activity. Supplementary worksheets enable teachers to tailor content to the needs of their own pupils, but there is a danger that the spirit duplicator becomes a substitute for spirited teaching and children face what has been described as 'death by a thousand work cards' (Wragg, 1978).

Interest is often easier to gain than to retain. Novel displays or demonstrations, stimulating questions or unusual statements can successfully 'hook' attention. Unless intending to give a lecture (a format only suited to academic work with highly motivated students), the teacher should aim to shift the focus of this attention from himself to some pupil-centred activity. This process will be helped and a purpose will be given to the lesson if this intention is clearly indicated in a brief outline at the start of the lesson, which tells the pupil what the lesson is going to be about and what he will be expected to do.

Readability of Materials

Can the pupil read at whatever level the material is presented? Does he have the vocabulary necessary to grasp new concepts? Are there too many long words and involved sentences? Children who are withdrawn from English lessons to receive remedial help with their reading are expected to deal with complicated texts in history, geography and science without any additional assistance in those subjects. Apart from the cognitive problems involved, children who are experiencing difficulties in reading may not be able to glean enough information to assimilate new concepts, unless some effort is made to provide simplified synopses and oral summaries of the content of difficult texts.

Matching the reading level of textbooks with the reading age of the children using them is not a difficult task. Harrison (1980) describes the various formulae which are available, explains how to apply them and advises which are most suitable for primary and secondary material. Particularly at the senior level, too little account is taken of whether pupils can read the books from which they are expected to work independently (Lunzer and Gardner, 1979).

Choosing new books may not be an available option. Even if this is the case, much can be done to help pupils cope with unsuitable textbooks containing reading matter beyond their normal level of comprehension. Attention can be directed to relevant paragraphs. Exercises can be simplified or easier activities substituted. Essential concepts can be illustrated by selecting key words which reflect the main ideas from a passage. These can be written up on the blackboard, explained and discussed before independent work starts. Every effort should be made to ensure that the pupil knows exactly what information to seek and where to find it. Gardner (1980) has coined the acronym DARTs (directed activities related to text) to describe this type of approach.

Clarity of Presentation

Even pupils who can read adequately sometimes need help in sorting out what they are expected to do. Clarity of presentation should remove any vagueness about the purpose of the lesson or the nature of the work anticipated from the pupils. Are assignments clear enough, so that each pupil knows exactly what is expected? Do some children give up because they do not know what to do? Do others go off on the wrong track, not because they cannot do the work, but because they get the instructions wrong?

Having settled the class into the lesson and cleared their minds of other topics, such as the previous lesson, by some quiet seat-work on his own subject, the teacher should introduce new work by giving a simple outline of his lesson plan. This should emphasise what the pupils will be expected to do during and after the teacher's talk, demonstration or film. It is essential to ensure that listening or watching should be active rather than passive. This can be achieved by setting a few questions to be answered or directing attention to important concepts, which are going to be introduced. This also gives an opportunity to check that children have the necessary materials for getting on with their work as soon as the teacher's part has finished.

Instructions should be clearly written on a part of the chalkboard reserved for this purpose, perhaps in a different colour from that used for summarising the lesson content, providing headings and spellings. Regular instructions relating to the presentation and the setting out of work may best be permanently displayed on a poster, with an example of what is required clearly visible.

Checks need to be made that instructions have been understood by asking individuals to repeat them. This should be done as pleasantly and patiently as possible, not with the intention of catching anybody out, but rather just to make sure they have got it right.

As work gets under way, the teacher needs to be around to help. If one person is stuck, a quiet personal explanation can be sufficient, but if several pupils are evidently puzzled, then it is best to stop everyone, get the attention of the whole class and repeat instructions, giving extra examples or further demonstrations, if necessary. It is useful to assume that for every pupil who appears to be stuck there is another who, though working with some appearance of confidence, would welcome the reassurance of a further explanation.

Difficulty of Tasks

Are tasks set at a level of difficulty which offers some measure of challenge, but also a chance of success? Do children get stuck and fail to complete their work? Do some children manage in class, but fail with homework? Martin and Lauridsen (1974) suggest that it sometimes appears as if schools set out to exacerbate failure by moving their less able pupils too rapidly through the curriculum. 'If a student is having trouble with simple addition, move the whole class ahead to fractions and leave him further and further behind.'

Thus tasks need to be set with the individual, rather than the class average, in mind. In the demonstration phase of the lesson, some children will need more time to answer questions or grasp ideas. Careful questioning should alert the teacher to any problems, and these can often be solved by giving further examples or restating an idea in simpler terms. Although it is necessary to beware of overelaboration slowing down the progress of the rest of the class, the greater danger is that somebody will 'get two, three steps behind and then it's too late' (Weber 1982).

During the practice phase, difficulties show up when children who clearly understand the instructions nevertheless get stuck. This may be a symptom of a problem which needs deeper diagnosis, but in the first instance emphasis should be placed on helping stragglers to keep up.

Sometimes this can be achieved by giving an extra clue or prompting a correct answer by narrowing the field of search: 'It's near London on the map' or 'Look at the second paragraph'. On other occasions, it is more appropriate to modify the assignment, cutting down the required amount of work or sidestepping the difficult problem for the time being. 'Just do the first ten' or 'Leave that question, go on to the next one'. For certain children work will need to be broken down into shorter segments with more frequent feedback, for example, marking every five sums instead of every twenty.

The technique for group teaching described as 'branching' is a very useful means of ensuring that work demands are related to a pupil's potential and capacity to respond. Grouping will also ease the arrangement of extra coaching or repetition of examples, without delaying the rest of the class.

If difficulties are encountered because children do not have the prerequisite skills, then arrangements need to be made for revision or reteaching of those skills. Often teachers assume that children have certain skills because these have been taught in previous years, but, although taught, the skills may not have been learnt or mastered. In the meantime, alternative easier work can be provided, while taking account of the problem by setting a more attainable target for the next session. It is useless, for example, to attempt long division if the short version has not been mastered.

Some children will be able to work competently enough, but only at a pace that leaves them adrift of their classmates. This may be due to distraction, through chatting with friends or being too interested in other people's work, instead of getting on with their own. In extreme cases, this may necessitate moving children away from the source of distraction. Usually a reminder of the need for concentration on the task in hand will suffice, particularly if the prohibition on discussion is only for a limited period. 'You may talk to your neighbour when you've both finished this exercise.'

It is important to ensure that work is completed as homework, if not within the lesson. However, this should not become too hefty an imposition on children who are working steadily, if rather slowly. In exceptional circumstances, losses may need to be cut by the abandonment of a particularly difficult exercise and its replacement by something easier. This should rarely happen once a teacher has had an opportunity to assess his pupils' abilities.

Homework should be set to reinforce learning that has taken place in school. It should provide further practice, rather than introduce new ideas. Children who might be able to manage with the assistance of the teacher can easily become confused when expected to cope with variations and 'surprises' on their own. For many children, the reassuring presence and support of the teacher is needed, if new learning is to be tackled successfully. When homework involves the collection and collation of information, pupils should be told which sources to consult, rather than be expected to find out for themselves. If preparatory reading is required, then it should be for a clearly indicated purpose with a framework provided by a short list of pertinent questions.

Marking System

The consequences as well as the conditions of learning contribute to the nature of the classroom environment. The way in which work is marked and rewarded will influence the climate for nurturing positive attitudes. Is marking on a personal or competitive basis? Do rewards for successful work sufficiently motivate the pupils? How often do individuals gain rewards?

Whether external examinations are involved or not, it is important that marks should be related to standards which give the learner a realistic perception of his own ability. However, this does not mean that the less able child should be constantly reminded of his inadequacy compared with other pupils. Competition can sometimes play a useful part in stimulating effort, but this can be related to individual targets, rather than comparative performances. The same rewards can be given for one child who gets five sums correct and another who gets ten correct, provided that in each case it is a 'personal best'.

It is sometimes helpful to separate marks for content and presentation. This enables the teacher to find something to praise, whether it is getting the idea or setting out the work. Written comments can soften the blow of a poor mark and show that effort and industry are appreciated as well as competence.

Whenever possible, correction should be an opportunity to improve a mark, rather than an imposition or punishment. 'Fair copy never won fresh interest' and it is better to give further practice with new though similar work, always assuming that the first attempt was a best effort; if not, then the mild punishment of repetition may be appropriate.

Successful work may bring its own rewards. Bruner (1966) describes 'intrinsic' motives for learning, which do not depend on rewards outside the instructional activity itself. Children work to satisfy their natural curiosity or for the sense of achievement which follows competent performance. They work for the pleasure of interaction with a well-liked teacher, often identifying with his attitudes and enthusiasms. They work also for the enjoyment of shared effort in being a member of a co-operative group. On the other hand, Skinner (1968) argues that learning depends not on the activity itself, but on the consequences which follow. Children work for 'extrinsic' motives such as praise, approval or more tangible reward, or they work to avoid unpleasant consequences such as disapproval or punishment.

Without taking sides in this continuing debate, the teacher may draw on either theory in developing a positive approach. What matters is the need for an accurate perception of what motivates particular pupils in particular lessons. It is also important that each individual has a regular opportunity of experiencing reward, whether in terms of self-esteem, the regard of others, or the enjoyment of pleasant consequences.

Encouragement and Momentum

The teacher's ability to convey positive expectations depends on efficient lesson-planning organisation and evaluation. It also depends on these activities being infused with 'encouragement'. Weber (1982) uses this term to describe 'an affirmation of belief in the pupil's potential and capacity to do better'. Enthusiasm could be considered as every teacher's second subject. It can be shown through interest in the subject matter and concern in setting interesting and stimulating work. It can also be demonstrated by enjoyment of the company of children and the ability to share a joke. It is encouragement which stops a teacher becoming defeatist or a class becoming demoralised.

If positive expectations are successfully conveyed, then pupils respond with an impetus and involvement which generates 'momentum'. Weber (1982) uses this term to describe that realisation of capacity for achievement which keeps people moving on their own, even when difficulties are encountered. Faced with repeated failure, pupils will inevitably lose momentum. To avoid this happening, teachers need to examine carefully their use of rewards and punishments.

4 REWARDS AND PUNISHMENTS

Implicitly or explicitly, all teachers use rewards and punishments. Even teachers who would vehemently reject the idea of giving prizes use praise, affection and attention in a rewarding way, and withdrawal of such favours can be as punishing, in its own way, as a hearty smack.

To use rewards and punishments effectively requires knowledge and judicious application of the principles of behaviour modification. Aid available from studies in this area may be rejected by teachers who consider this approach to be manipulative and mechanistic. There is an unfortunate impression that behavioural psychologists are invariably white-coated scientists, most used to doing unpleasant things to helpless laboratory rats and inclined to treat people the same way. Even when not perceived in this unfair and unfavourable light, behaviourism is seen as a complicated, time-consuming business, heavily dependent on stopwatch, clipboard and technical jargon. Although many accounts of behavioural modification with children are written as academic papers by psychologists for psychologists, their implications are none the less relevant to teachers. Approached with common sense, they provide useful guidance on the application of rewards and punishments in the classroom.

Essentially, the behavioural approach argues that the single most important factor in learning a behaviour is what happens immediately following that behaviour. Pleasant consequences are most likely to reinforce the behaviour and make it more likely to happen again. For teachers, this means defining what they want children to do, then organising classroom events so that pleasant consequences follow when they do it.

Wallace and Kauffman (1978) emphasise the importance of having a planned rather than haphazard programme for this 'Systematic arrangement of environmental events which produces a specific change in observable behaviour'. The key words here are 'systematic', 'specific' and 'observable' and, though much will depend on the particular situaation, the basic elements of a behaviour-modification approach to group or individual management will always involve description, observation, reward and evaluation.

Description

Most teachers' ideas of the behaviour they want their pupils to display start with rather vague constructs such as 'working hard' or 'not disturbing others'. Before thinking about how to provide pleasant consequences for these behaviours, it is necessary for teacher and class to understand precisely what the required behaviour is. In other words, to know what observable activities constitute the occasion for reward.

'Working', for example, might be defined in terms of a list of activities such as listening to, looking at or answering questions from the teacher, writing answers in a book or following instructions from the blackboard. 'Not disturbing others' might be classified as refraining from such activities as grabbing, knocking over or destroying other children's books, assignments or equipment, calling out, pushing, scraping or banging desks.

Whether working with groups or individuals, it is important not only to be specific about the description of desired and undesired behaviour, but also to be realistic about how much can be achieved. Success is more likely to be achieved if a few problems are tackled at a time, rather than trying to apply the strategy to a variety of different behaviours. Thus for a class, there might be few simple rules or conventions, observation of which will be rewarded. With an individual, however many and varied his problems, treatment should focus on one or two items, selected as being most critical.

Another aspect of describing and defining behaviour is the need to accentuate the positive by placing emphasis on the performance of good behaviour, rather than the avoidance of bad. Attention should not be drawn to anti-social activities by offering children a reward for not doing them. It is much better to reward some worthwhile behaviour incompatible with the cause of annoyance. Praise should be given for raising the hand and waiting for permission to speak, rather than requests made for children not to call out. Carter (1972) suggests that when faced by children doing something which they do not want, they should ask themselves: 'what would I like them to do instead?'

Consistently attending to desired behaviour, while ignoring undesired behaviour, is a simple but highly effective demonstration of this approach (Becker *et al.*, 1967). Not reacting to a nuisance is rarely enough on its own, because the other children will attend, even if the teacher does not. Providing a more acceptable means of giving attention is an important aspect of selecting a 'target' behaviour. However, Clarizio (1976) suggests that it is always worth considering whether misbehaviour is important enough to warrant intervention. Teachers should ask themselves just what will happen, if they merely ignore the source of the trouble. Frequently, the reaction of the members of the class will be the most crucial factor.

If it is decided that 'planned ignoring' will not be enough, then in choosing a target behaviour that will be encouraged teachers should seek something that will contribute to academic or social adjustment. Usually this will involve providing some specific work to do.

Description therefore involves describing precisely what is causing the problem and exactly what would alleviate it. After defining 'what' is happening, the next question is 'how often' does it happen.

Observation

Some teachers experience difficulty in accepting a behavioural approach, because of its apparent insistence on a highly technical system of recording. Again, this reflects the origin of much of the literature as scientific reports on tightly controlled experiments. The jargon of interval recording and percentage rates per minute does make the whole business sound more complicated than need be. It is not that these techniques are intrinsically difficult, but, particularly when associated with timers, logs, charts and graphs, they do seem likely to introduce an undue additional amount of paraphernalia into a teacher's busy life. There is little enough time for lesson planning, preparation of materials and marking work, yet some measurement is essential if progress is to be monitored.

The simplest and most useful measure is counting how frequently something happens in each lesson. Obviously, as with describing and defining behaviours, it is best to concentrate attention in this case on one or two individuals or actions. This will provide a 'baseline' or starting line indicating, say, how often a child calls out or how many times desk lids are banged before treatment is commenced. This data can then be used to check the effectiveness or otherwise of whatever reinforcement is given.

Even before treatment starts, measurement can be useful in providing information about the nature of a problem. Is it sufficiently serious to merit outside help in the form of disciplinary support for the teacher or therapeutic guidance for the child? If so, it will help attract that assistance if the teacher can indicate the number of times other children have been hit, the frequency of interrruptions per lesson or the amount of unfinished work.

Often the act of counting misbehaviours will itself provide either reassurance that the problem is not as bad as it seemed or an explanation of what might appear to be irrational or unpredictable behaviour. It may be revealed that apparently constant fighting only occurs with one or two children who incite these outbursts by provocative teasing. Seemingly senseless calling out may, on closer examination, be clearly designed to break the flow of the lesson and irritate the teacher. Assumed laziness may be related to genuine lack of competence or understanding in tackling certain subjects. In each case, there is still a problem to be resolved, but its dimensions become clearly more manageable.

Sometimes objective recording will demonstrate that the problem was not nearly so bad as it felt subjectively. Actually finding out how often misbehaviour or distraction does really occur helps teachers maintain a sense of proportion. Young teachers are especially likely to exaggerate the importance of comparatively minor incidents. Defining and counting particular misbehaviours can demonstrate that these do not amount to a serious challenge to authority.

Another welcome side-effect of 'baseline data collection' is the way that sometimes the very act of recording produces a modification in behaviour. Gnagey (1981) recounts the story of a teacher who designed an experiment to stop children slouching in their seats. She started to mark down each time a child slipped down in a seat. By the second day the class had cottoned on to the fact that sitting up straight was important to this teacher and 'slouching' had virtually ceased. It was a collapse of the stout experimenter, perhaps, but this anecdote illustrates an effect which is welcome in the classroom, if not in the laboratory or clinic. Although it detracts from experimental validity, awareness that behaviour is being observed and recorded may well have an immediate beneficial effect As Gnagey concludes, 'regardless of the horror stories you may have heard about students defying teachers, most pupils will do what you ask of them if it is clear and reasonable'.

Reward

Traditionally, school discipline has been more concerned with punishment than reward. It is not surprising, therefore, that some teachers feel a system of discipline based primarily on positive reinforcement is a sign of weakness, if not an admission of defeat. Others would argue that, if not yet ready to love learning for its own sake, pupils should be sufficiently motivated by respect or liking for their teacher.

Perhaps because much of its basis in research has been concerned with extremely disturbed or retarded behaviour, positive reinforcement is seen only in terms of immediate tangible reward, inappropriate to the normal classroom. However, Neisworth and Smith (1973) describe a reinforcement hierarchy which descends from self-generated satisfaction, such as pride in a job well done, through self-managed reinforcement, such as going out for the evening only after homework has been completed, to the management of reinforcement by others, intangibly in the form of social approval or praise or tangibly in the form of sweets, money or permission to take part in some enjoyed activity.

Positive reinforcement can be seen as a series of activities directed towards developing self-control and working upwards through this hierarchy. Although aiming towards self-management and working for motives of self-esteem, with children the starting point is usually making praise contingent on socially approved behaviours. From this level, it may be necessary to resort to more tangible reward, not out of desperation, but out of recognition that this is the most effective way to get rapid results.

Positive reinforcement occurs when the events that follow a behaviour strengthen its frequency, duration or intensity. It is thus what happens following the administration of a reinforcer, which determines whether it is positive. Whatever the teacher's intention, if the desired behaviour is not increased, then the reward is insufficiently motivating. Teachers may provide what they consider to be a variety of pleasant consequences for good work, but the quantity and quality of that work will not improve unless the pupils share the teachers' view of the desirability of the offered reward. Choosing appropriate rewards and a suitable system for their delivery are the most difficult aspects of behaviour modification in the classroom. Two techniques which help are the system of 'token economy' for groups and 'contingency contracting' for individuals.

Token economies

In the real world, money is a token which is later exchanged for goods or services; similarly, points or stars can be used as tokens which, though having no value in themselves, can later be exchanged for more potent reinforcers. This system has the attraction for the teacher that it gives prompt recognition to good work or appropriate behaviour, without the disruption to normal routine which could result from having to arrange an immediate reward. It also means that children who may be working for different incentives or towards different targets can be dealt with at the same time. A variety of 'back up' reinforcers can be provided, for which tokens may be exchanged or certain activities made contingent on gaining a required number of points.

Once again, it must be stressed that the teacher's view of what constitutes a 'potent reinforcer' may differ from the child's. Discussion with the class will often produce novel, but sensible ideas. The following items and activities have all been used as part of token economies, although their suitability will depend on the age-group of the children and their practicability in particular schools.

Food is undoubtedly a powerful reinforcer. Sweets, chocolates and crisps are certainly accepted with alacrity, even by older children. There may be reservations about using this form of reward, on grounds of dental hygiene as well as financial stringency. Fruit provides an alternative which is better for the teeth, if not the pocket.

Drink — in the form of access to adult beverages such as tea or coffee at break times — is likely to be a very effective reinforcer for older children. Its provision, together with fruit juices and possibly other soft drinks, can present organisational problems, but usually children will be only too pleased to manage this for themselves. The sense of belonging to an exclusive 'brew club' will only enhance the attraction of this form of reinforcement.

Discreet supervision is essential for this or other forms of 'club' activity which involve staying in the classroom at break or lunch time. Congenial activities, such as playing board games or listening to music, can all too easily degenerate into aimless messing about. This can lead to damage to furniture and equipment, which makes what was intended to be a rewarding and pleasurable session into an occasion for recrimination. If this can be avoided without depriving the teacher of some well-deserved relaxation, then 'staying in' can be a most effective reward. It is puzzling that many teachers still use the threat of 'keeping in' at playtime to try to make children work harder. In the winter months, older children will do a great deal to avoid the bare and uninviting playground.

Another pleasant consequence enjoyed by most pupils is the arrangement whereby some part of a lesson can be used for less formal pastimes. An example which might be appropriate at many ages includes being allowed to use particularly attractive and specially reserved art materials such as poster paints or felt tips. Another example might be access to a comic or magazine section of the class library. A suitable collection can rapidly be acquired with contributions from the pupils themselves or from the children of a teacher's friends who are often happy to bequeath a hoard of old comics which they have finally outgrown.

Privileges such as taking messages, tidying the room, preparing displays or other monitorial functions are usually valued by younger children. With older groups, the opportunity to complete homework in school time is highly prized. Depending on the attitude of colleagues, the teacher may need to limit this particular privilege to doing homework set by himself!

It is often not essential for tokens to be actually exchanged for privileges. It may suffice to make access to them available, provided a target number of points has been gained. The key feature of the behavioural approach is to make positive reinforcement contingent on appropriate behaviour. Therefore a token system must be regulated in such a manner that children are not excluded from a choice of rewards.

In some cases, a competitive element may be appropriate with prizes for the best weekly individual or team totals. Though often derided, 'house points' do have an effect, particularly with younger children. As rewards, house points can be linked to class points with an exchange rate geared to an appropriate amount of work.

All too often traditional house points are awarded in a vague and arbitrary way, which serves only to confuse rather than motivate. Children should know that when they reach a certain cumulative total of class points, they will gain a house point. What that total will be depends on the rating given to a house point in particular schools. In some cases it should be the equivalent of one day or one lesson's average work, in other schools it will equate to something more like a week's steady effort. What matters most is the fact that it can be seen as an attainable target for all children, rather than the preserve of the brightest and the best behaved.

The token economy is likely to suffer from many of the same problems as the real economy. It is therefore vital for the teacher to be prepared for them.

Inflation is not a serious problem, in this context. Children quite enjoy attaining astronomic totals, though these can be kept in check by having a fresh start at frequent intervals. This will also stop hoarding if reinforcers are being sold for tokens, rather than provided if targets have been reached.

Forgery and stealing are more likely to cause trouble. Both can be avoided by careful choice of the method of giving tokens. Either the teacher needs to keep his own record or to organise distribution in such a way that any irregularities can soon be spotted. It might, for example, be arranged that every ten red tokens are exchanged for a blue, every five blues for a green and so on. Though time-consuming, such systems give extra opportunities for linking praise with the award of points.

This process of associating or 'pairing' praise with giving reward should help children to learn to value approval as a source of reinforcement in itself. Indeed the points themselves may become little more than an amusement, which may be dispensed with or continued according to the wishes of the class. If a token economy is continued over a lengthy period of time, it is vital to maintain interest by introducing flexibility and novelty into the system. This might be done by having 'sales' or 'special offers', when the token 'price' of certain reinforcers is reduced for a limited period and offering additional incentives or extra prizes in particular weeks. On the production, as opposed to the sales management side, bonuses can be given for extra effort with double points for working after an initial target has been reached. On some days, extra points may be awarded for tackling certain more difficult tasks.

Introducing a token-economy system needs to be done in a sufficiently light-hearted and light-handed manner for wrangles to be avoided. Sceptical children and staff can be gradually drawn into participation, if they see others enjoying the activity. Discussion before starting the new approach can help identify suitable reinforcers and a format for the delivery and recording of tokens that is fitting to the age of the pupils and the type of school. Basically, token economy in the classroom should be seen as an enjoyable game, rather than a control system. If the teacher plays the game with enthusiasm, the class will follow suit. If the system becomes a heavy, rigid routine, it will fail.

Contingency Contracting

As not infrequently happens in educational psychology, contingency contracting is an elaborate term adopted to describe a simple process. It means that an agreement is reached between teacher and child that certain behaviours or performances will be rewarded in a particular way. What have previously been uncertain events, such as the amount of work from the pupil or the response from the teacher, become formally recognised.

Contingency management can be applied to groups; for example, the teacher only dismisses a row of children, when all are sitting quietly.

The main attraction of this approach, however, is for working with individuals, who will benefit from an explicit statement of the behaviour expected from them and the effect it is likely to have. In some cases, this statement can be accompanied by the formality of a written contract, stating exactly what the child and teacher will do and signed by both. In the normal classroom, a verbal contract will usually suffice. Although a written statement will help each side remember the terms of their deal, signed commitment ought to be reserved for important and exceptional agreements.

Although using this approach is a more informal way, the teacher can benefit from applying a principle that has been found to work in arranging contracts with more seriously disturbed children. Known as the Premack Principle, after the psychologist by whom it was formulated, this states that: 'Any higher frequency behaviour that is contingent upon a lower frequency behaviour is likely to increase the rate of the lower frequency behaviour.' In other words, more preferred activities can be used to reinforce less preferred activities. More colloquial expressions of this principle, sometimes also referred to as 'Grandma's rule', state: 'Eat your greens before you get your pudding', or 'Wash the dishes before you go out to play'.

Careful observation is needed to make sure which classroom activities are preferred, but if this is done, then some academic activities can be used to reinforce others. For children who enjoy reading, this might follow written work, or in some cases familiar mechanical arithmetic could follow work on more demanding problems. Where drawing, tracing or colouring are involved in lessons, these should usually follow written or oral questions.

Preferred leisure or recreational activities can be made contingent upon the performance of academic assignments; Homme (1970) suggests that such rewards need to be immediate and frequent. Particularly when starting this approach 'little but often' should be the guideline. In effect, there may need to be a whole series of mini-contracts establishing a routine that 'first you work and then you play'. However, although tests should be small and simple to perform, they should contribute something useful towards the child's development and provide him with a sense of accomplishment. Contracts should involve earning a reward for doing something worth while, rather than receiving a bribe for not doing something. In this way, the teacher is not trying to train acquiescence or obedience, but is aiming from the start to move the child from dependent to independent effort.

Evaluation

No intervention will immediately resolve all disciplinary problems. However, behaviour modification should begin to have some effect within a fairly short period of time. Somewhere between five and ten sessions should be enough to provide information for the assessment and, if necessary, the adaptation of a particular programme.

Ideally, behaviour is specified and counted in the phases of description and it should have continued to be noted during the treatment phase. There is no real alternative to this way of providing sound evidence of success or failure; however, it is undoubtedly time-consuming and realistically might be reserved for dealing with the most intractable individual problems. Some factual record of the amount of work done or the number of misdemeanours committed is clearly needed. This can be provided by having a recording or observation session at regular intervals, rather than every lesson. One advantage of the token system is the way in which it provides its own built-in evaluation. If the system is working, then children are attaining or exceeding their targets.

In a broader sense, teachers also need to evaluate a behavioural approach in terms of their own objectives. Is the system making teaching more pleasant and enjoyable? Is the investment of time in behavioural engineering producing a good return in academic achievement and social competence?

Punishment

If positive efforts are not working, then it may be necessary to resort to punishment. This is an effective way of changing behaviour, but teachers need to be well aware of its unfortunate side-effects. Punishment provides an inappropriate model of behaviour. Children may learn that you get your own way by hurting other people and copy adults in throwing their weight around in solving personal problems. Especially whn physical punishment is involved, aggression may be displaced and, though compliance in the classroom is obtained, other children suffer in the playground (Vargas, 1977).

There may well be emotional side-effects which can be more devastating than the behaviour which provoked the punishment. Anxiety reactions may cause children to 'clam up' (Carter, 1972). Mutual aversion can build up to the extent that positive interaction becomes impossible, and teacher and pupil become trapped in a series of clashes developing into a spiral of dislike.

Although punishment gets quick results, these tend to be short-lived. The punished behaviour may only be suppressed in the actual presence of the 'punishing agent' (Buckley and Walker, 1970). This phenomenon is disconcerting for young teachers, who find that though heads and senior teachers support them by punishing children referred for misbehaviour, on their return the offenders rapidly resume their provocation.

Sometimes being punished merely teaches children to avoid getting caught. This can add to problems, and sometimes lying, cheating and even truancy may be tried to escape retribution for an initially less serious offence (Becker, Engelmann and Thomas, 1975).

For these reasons, it can be seen that although punishment works, it does not mean that it should be used. There are also ethical and legal considerations concerning the use of harsh, intense punishment. Perhaps the greatest shortcoming of punishment is the observation that, though it may stop a bad behaviour, it will not start a good one. None the less, there are times when behaviour is so disruptive, persistent or dangerous, that priority must be given to putting a stop to it in the interests of safety, security and sanity.

Actual physical danger to other children, whether from aggressive bullying or boisterous disregard for the safety of others, is an example of a situation where punishment may well need to be used. However, there are many less distinct areas. Some children do test how far they can go and the establishment of clear boundaries regarding tolerable behaviour will give security to the rest of the class as well as the troublemaker himself. There are also times when teachers find that certain behaviours, though not dangerous or threatening, are in Churchill's phrase 'something up with which they will not put'. Instant reaction is rarely rational, but it is sometimes right. Provided that teachers do not find this response being triggered too easily or too often, it can be considered as a safety valve, preserving mental health and well-being.

Aversive Consequences

Punishment either involves making something unpleasant happen or removing some reward or privilege. The main problem with the aversive consequences available in school is the fact that they are all likely to be administered some considerable time after the event and there is a good deal of evidence to show that immediacy is an important element in making punishment effective (Poteet, 1973). Canings, impositions and detentions are nowadays received so long after the precipitating crime, that appreciation of cause and effect is lost. Suspensions and exclusions suffer even more from the delays occasioned by necessary processes of parental notification.

For the classroom teacher, lines and detentions are the most unpleasant consequences he is likely to be able to impose on his pupils. As with positive reinforcement, careful observation is needed to see whether intended results are being achieved. If the teacher finds that he is giving lengthier impositions and more detentions as the term progresses, then, however unpleasant he may think them, these consequences are not being effective as punishments. It is tempting in such circumstances to resort to would-be exemplary sentences, but apart from the effect on the actual sufferer, imposing very harsh punishment only heightens drama and tension. Better by far to hold to the principle of imposing as mild a punishment as is compatible with the seriousness of the offence. If aversive consequences must be used, it may help to establish a totting up procedure rather like that used in relation to motoring offences. Three minor impositions within a certain period of time could lead to an inevitable detention, though, as with the magistrate's power to disqualify, the heavier penalty could be imposed for certain serious offences irrespective of the number of 'endorsements'.

The punishment most easily imposed by the classroom teacher is stopping some pleasant activity or privilege. Jones and Jones (1981) describe 'activity curtailment', as they term it, as a natural way of altering children's behaviour, 'used since time began' and requiring no special forms of record keeping from the teacher. However, care needs to be taken to ensure that the activity to be curtailed is actually sufficiently prized by the child for its withdrawal to act as a punishment. This form of punishment can be most appropriate as a group contingency. Missing out on storytime or part of the lesson reserved for quizzes, guessing games and other forms of relaxation can generate an amount of peer-group pressure towards behavioural conformity. Such tactics should always be used cautiously, because resentment can easily backfire and previously pleasant parts of the lesson can become bones of contention.

Response Cost

If a points system is used, then taking points away can be an effective means of demonstrating that certain behavioural responses will 'cost' their performer something, in terms of reducing the amount of positive reinforcement which he receives. Two problems can arise, if teachers adopt this form of punishment. It adds to the complication of running a token economy, because the teacher has to monitor inappropriate as well as appropriate behaviour, and it can generate negative attitudes to the system as a whole.

The difficulties involved in administraion can be reduced by having only a few clearly defined offences for which points can be lost. It can be argued that response cost provides pupils with essential feedback showing what they should not do, as well as what they should do. Discussing which behaviours should lose points provides an opportunity to establish the rationale behind the application of sanctions. Gnagey (1981) suggests reasoning matched to the cognitive level of the children involved can have a powerful influence on the effectiveness of punishment.

Negative reactions can be reduced by ensuring that deductions are made in a manner which is not vindictive or provocative. Though reasoning may be helpful in establishing the need for rules, moralising at the time when they are administered is not helpful. It is more likely to be interpreted by the child as 'rubbing it in' and therefore may ignite, rather than defuse, a potentially explosive situation. Used sparingly, response cost can provide an element of just retribution and fairness, which indicates the framework of security within which a more positive approach can work best. In general, it is best to give points to reward good behaviour, rather than remove points to punish bad behaviour. It is better to give a bonus for punctuality than to impose a penalty for being late.

Another form of punishment in which a cost is imposed for misbehaviour is 'time out'. This American term describes a procedure whereby pupils are isolated for a short period of time. It may involve physical isolation by removal from the classroom or sending to a quiet corner of the class. It can also take the form of social exclusion from certain activities. In theory, the child is being withdrawn from a reinforcing situation and the whole technique depends on the assumption that the lesson is sufficiently attractive for the child to want to rejoin it as soon as possible (Leach and Raybould, 1977).

In the ordinary classroom, 'time out' is fraught with procedural difficulties. Sending a child out of the room is rarely in itself a punishment. Corridors and cloakrooms are full of interesting distractions. Taking a child to the head ought to be an ultimate deterrent, rather than a tactical option. Bare, blank rooms or cubicles are rarely available and though improvisation with screened-off corners or carrels may be possible, this does not provide the complete isolation from rein-forcement and involvement which is an essential feature of this approach.

The sheer drama, potential for dispute and disruption to normal routine may even be welcomed by children intent on serious mischief. Although it may well be effective with small groups in special circum-stances, time out does not appear to offer an effective and applicable sanction in the ordinary school.

Avoiding Unofficial Reinforcement

However stern the intended sanction, teachers need to be careful that its application does not produce unforeseen and unintended conse-quences. Unofficial reinforcement can maintain undesired behaviours even in the face of harsh official punishment. Excitement and status are more important to some children than any unpleasantness that may also result.

Pupils who find that they can easily provoke angry outbursts from the teacher may exploit this ability to undermine a teacher's dignity and authority. There are times when a teacher needs to express his anger, but there is a thin line between rage and despair; he may stim-ulate fear or only amusement and derision. Even if compliance is gained in the classroom, the troublemaker enjoys a certain kudos in the play-ground. Lessons can easily become battles of wits, and although teachers usually win such power struggles, these conflicts sap energy and sour rela-tionships.

If punishment must be employed, then it should be administered in a calm and matter-of-fact manner, free from recrimination. It should follow a clear and unequivocal warning to terminate the undesired be-haviour. If at all possible, this warning should be quietly addressed to the individual and accompanied by advice about what should be done instead. This mild reprimand may be sufficient in itself to stop the mis-behaviour; if not, then the threatened punishment must follow. Repeated warnings lapse easily into ineffectual nagging. Therefore, before giving a warning, the teacher needs to be clear in his own mind that the behaviour is bad enough to deserve punishment if it continues.

Perhaps the most dangerous unofficial reinforcement is the way in which punishment rewards the teacher. If successful, it immediately suppresses the unwanted behaviour and compels the obedience of the child. Sometimes socially reinforced by staffroom attitudes, the teacher resorts more and more frequently to punishment, whatever his ethical views about it. Efficient punishment is habit forming. Once addicted, teachers will find it harder to develop a more pleasant and positive approach.

5 HELPING COLLEAGUES COPE

This chapter is mainly addressed to senior teachers, heads of department or others who have responsibility for guiding less experienced colleagues. It is largely an expansion of an earlier consideration of the consultant role of the remedial teacher (Smith, 1982). It is also a review and drawing together of themes developed earlier in this book and an illustration of how they might be applied within the context of one teacher helping another to become a more effective classroom manager. Specific references are made to earlier chapters and these should be used to expand points made more briefly here.

Unvoiced Questions

Marsh and Price (1980) point out that when one teacher seeks help from another, there are certain unvoiced questions in his mind. They suggest that consultant teachers need to bear these questions in mind when responding to a call for advice about classroom management.

Will You Listen: Really Listen?

Good communication starts with effective listening. A colleague with a problem wants a fair hearing, rather than a pat answer. Too ready a response may be interpreted as an attempt to brush aside the teacher's own perception of the situation. Martin (1980) gives a useful resumé of the listening skills by which interest and concern are shown through expression, gesture and tone of response. Attentive silence can be supported by maintaining eye contact, and giving a confirmatory nod of the head at appropriate stages of the narrative. Often people are encouraged to talk by what might be called 'listening noises', such as 'Yes . . . really . . . I see . . . uh, uh . . . mm . . . ' By repeating or paraphrasing key phrases or sentences, the listener shows that he is following the speaker's line of argument.

'I haven't got the time to spend with one child' might, for example, become: 'The group is too large for you to give this child the individual attention he needs'. The listening phase should conclude with a brief summary by the listener of the speaker's case. This enables both parties to check that the intended message has been received and understood. 'You think that problems arise with this boy, because he can't read well enough to cope with the textbooks in your subject.'

The good listener should avoid finishing other people's sentences, guessing the outcome of a line of thought or interrupting. Rephrasing and summarising should be undertaken as aids to memory, rather than opportunities for advice at this stage.

It is much more difficult to follow Martin's undoubtedly excellent suggestions than it sounds, when advice is sought in a crowded staff-room rather than a formal counselling session. None the less, these are valuable guidelines for helping consultant teachers demonstrate that they are *really* listening and taking seriously the viewpoint being expressed to them. This is particularly important in view of the next question likely to be in the mind of the teacher asking for advice.

Does Asking for Assistance Imply Incompetence?

Teachers may feel that asking for advice about classroom management implies some admission of weakness on their part. This feeling is likely to be reinforced if a request for help is met by a glib answer. It is important, therefore, that a consultant teacher should be able to establish empathy with colleagues. Empathy requires the ability to convince another person that you know how he feels. Many teachers who are themselves superb practitioners of classroom management make poor consultants or advisers, because they lack this ability to see things from another person's perspective.

A teacher who is already feeling inadequate and doubtful about his self-image as a competent professional will not be helped by easy or didactic answers. Even when the solution is obvious to the more experienced teacher, the temptation to show off should be avoided, and advice should be phrased in a manner which shows respect for colleagues, by suggesting, rather than dictating, what they ought to do. 'Have you tried separating those two children?' 'How about providing simpler work for the less able children?' 'What worked for me was reading through the problem sums . . . '

Will You Tell the Boss?

Another source of anxiety, which may deter some teachers from seeking help, is the fear that word of their inefficiency will be passed on to higher authority. A tendency to gloat over the disciplinary misfortunes of other teachers is an unworthy, but not unknown, characteristic of some members of the teaching profession. It is entirely out of place in any teacher who hopes to encourage colleagues to treat him as a consultant on techniques of classroom management.

In an area with so much 'ego involvement', a teacher wants reassurance that advice can be sought in confidence, without his difficulties being further publicised. Head teachers may feel that they can provide this sort of private comfort and guidance, without it adversely affecting their overall judgement of a teacher's capability. However, there is an understandable, though doubtless unfair, suspicion on the part of junior staff that, in dealing with 'the boss', anything they say may be taken down and used in reference against them!

The consultant teacher therefore needs to be an intermediary figure, whose involvement will be not exactly secretive, but at least self-effacing with confidentiality assured as far as possible.

Does 'Help' Mean Extra Work for Me?

Another concern, which may prevent some teachers from asking for assistance, is a natural unwillingness to add further complications to an already difficult task. Unless suggested remedies are simple and backed by support in their implementation, there will be a reluctance to bring problems forward.

Teachers are unlikely to turn for help to a colleague, if they suspect this will result in their being involved in an elaborate and time-consuming behaviour-modification programme or urged to read a long list of books on psycholinguistics. Initially, at least, the teacher with a problem is looking for relief rather than re-education. This may be supplied by withdrawing an individual pupil or providing additional help in the classroom. Actual intervention by the consultant teacher will be discussed further in a later part of this chapter, but for the moment the main point emphasised by this question and the next one, is the need for advice to be simple, direct and practical.

Can Anything be Done Quickly, which will Make a Difference Now?

Some problems will need considerable investigation before a long-term solution can be found. However, to the teacher seeking help, in-depth analysis matters less than action, which can make working with a particular class or individual child easier and pleasanter within the next few lessons.

Hawisher and Calhoun (1978) suggest that advice on immediate 'instructional adjustment' should focus on mode, time, space and grouping. The mode of teaching might be changed to allow more verbal than written work, if the problem is related to the expression of ideas. Alternatively, it might be appropriate to require more individual written work, if problems concern disruptive noisiness during discussion. The time allowed for completing tasks may be too short for some pupils or too long for the class as a whole. Workpace may need to be adjusted by providing a quiet corner or separate alcove for distractable pupils. Some children work better in pairs or groups than on their own, but these arrangements need careful planning and frequent review.

At this stage, advice is best framed as a series of alternative approaches, rather than offering a simple solution. This will help preserve the self-esteem of the teacher seeking advice by involving him in making choices and decisions. In effect, the adviser requires an agenda for discussion, which will provide a framework for gleaning further information and for giving pertinent advice. The following five questions and four topics should help formulate that agenda.

Five Questions to Ask

Asking the following questions will help the consultant teacher frame a rapid response, which should lead to a prompt improvement in classroom atmosphere and teaching performance. They need to be addressed tactfully and not necessarily in this precise form, but taken together they cover the main causes of classroom friction.

Have You Told Them?

Has the teacher given instructions which are clear enough, explicit enough and frequent enough to make sure that all the children know exactly what is required of them. Slow learners especially may need reminding about methods of presentation and ways of tackling problems.

More trouble arises from confusion over what to do, rather than over blank refusal to do it. As Lovitt (1977) points out, once children know what we want them to do, they usually do it. Discussing the clarity of presentation of lesson content and instructions can be an important first step in providing useful advice (Chapter 3).

Have You Showed Them?

Has the task been demonstrated and examples worked through, not only with the whole group, but also individually with pupils who are having difficulty? Some children will need additional help, even when instructions are clear enough. Often a technique or idea may be grasped one week, but forgotten or misapplied the next. Working through extra examples at a child's desk can often reveal the reason for apparently thoughtless mistakes.

At all levels of ability, some model for the way work should be set out and presented can establish what are the required standards and prevent misunderstanding. Unless they are given such a clear and concrete demonstration of what is required, many less able children will simply not 'see' what the teacher wants. Often teachers do not realise how many mistakes derive from disability, rather than disobedience and discussion of the difficulty of tasks may be helpful (Chapter 3).

Have You Listened to Them?

This question can be considered in two contexts. Listening can involve hearing children 'talk through' the steps they take in tackling a problem or it can involve inviting comment from the class as a whole on the way in which lessons are conducted.

At the individual level, problems in arithmetic, for example, can be revealed by getting a pupil to describe aloud exactly what he is doing. In this way, the teacher may find that the pupil is 'carrying' the units instead of the tens and an apparently wayward answer becomes explicable. In other subjects, discussing and amending 'draft' answers can prevent 'daft' answers by giving the teacher insight into misunderstandings and misperceptions.

Readiness to invite comment and consumer participation in planning and evaluating lessons is a way of displaying openness that is much appreciated by pupils. It must be undertaken with some forethought. Questions about lesson content should be specific rather than general. Anything that approximates to an enquiry like 'What do you think of it, so far?' will invite the now time-honoured response. However, questions such as 'Do you want another explanation of Boyle's Law?' or 'Were there enough examples of quadratic equations? Would you like more practice?' can provide valuable feedback to the teacher on aspects of presentation (Chapter 3).

Have You Praised Them?

The frequent use of praise is the quickest and most effective route to promoting a positive atmosphere in the classroom. Very often the reason teachers seek advice from colleagues is because a negative atmosphere has soured relationships with their pupils. They have become trapped in a vicious circle of complaint and criticism, prompting surliness and disaffection which results in further antagonism.

It is not easy in this situation for some teachers to find occasion to praise some children. Initially, it may be useful to suggest that easier tasks be set so that children almost inevitably succeed, giving the teacher an opportunity to 'catch them being good'. In this way the malign circle of reactions will be replaced by a benign one, in which praise and pleasure promote satisfaction and self-esteem.

Choosing activities which are success-prone without being so patently simple that the teacher's tactic becomes obvious is a skilled job. It requires judgement about the suitability of subject matter and the selection of lesson content (Chapter 3), which calls for an application of professional competence in the area of subject knowledge, rather than personal management.

From the consultant teacher's viewpoint, this shift of emphasis is wholly advantageous. It moves discussion from an area in which there is a poor self-image as an inadequate class manager to one where there is a sense of confidence as a knowledgeable specialist. Advice should always be aimed at developing strengths, rather than revealing weaknesses.

Have You Realised How Good You Are?

Colleagues, too, need praise. Teachers should be encouraged to see their difficulties within the context of general success. Whatever is going wrong with one class or individual, there will be other times and places where things are going right. Examining their own more successful lessons and relationships should give clues to adaptations needed in the problem situations.

Sometimes lessons which work well with brighter pupils do not work well with less able scholars, because the level of readability of materials is too high (Chapter 3). Some classes run smoothly while everyone is kept busy with individual work, but present problems when pupils are required to sit listening to a lecture for any length of time. Alteration to the variety and pace of lesson content may provide the answer (Chapter 1). Difficulties may often arise at particular stages of a lesson, and this might indicate that more attention should be given to planning that part of the lesson. It may be that lessons start well, but conclude badly. If so, what is making the difference? Very often it is simply the fact that the teacher has prepared the beginning, but not the ending of the lesson (Chapter 1).

With most individuals there are periods of amicability, which may be upset by particular incidents. Examining these may show the teacher that certain types of disciplinary intervention are more effective than others. With some children 'planned ignoring' or attempted 'signal interference' may be a waste of time, but 'interest boosting' and 'hurdle help' can avoid the need for possibly counter-productive punishment (Chapter 2). Teachers may feel that with some pupils they just do not enjoy any periods of amicability on which to build. If so, then they should be encouraged to look at those pupils with whom they do get on and consider how far it is their own approach or method of dealing with the pupil which contributes to the success of the relationship. Can some element of this approach be transferred?

By discussing problems in a way which stresses what a teacher does right, rather than what he does wrong, the consultation should become a positive and self-enhancing experience and thus one most likely to be repeated.

Four Topics for Discussion

Thus far the consultant teacher's agenda for discussion has contained questions related to what might be considered the general strategy of classroom management. Attention should also be given to what might be termed tactical aspects. Four areas of lesson organisation which may spark off conflict, particularly with less able children, are standards of work, provision of support when difficulties are encountered, the marking system and the use of rewards.

Standards of Work

Are standards set which are related to the learner's competence? Are the teacher's expectations based on a realistic appraisal of what the learner can do? Sometimes specialist-subject teachers are just not aware of the problems that some of their pupils have with basic literacy skills. In schools where 'remedial' has simply become another euphemism for the bottom stream, it is often not realised that many other children in the average-ability band have specific problems with reading or writing or spelling which affect their work across a range of subjects. Other children, though reasonably competent in these areas and by no means mentally retarded, do not easily grasp new concepts or cannot analyse and understand them sufficiently well to store new ideas in their memory so that they can be retrieved when required.

Further help may be needed from the school's remedial department, in the form of individual testing, extra coaching or adaptation of materials. However, at this stage discussion can be based on questions concerning subject matter and difficulty of tasks (Chapter 3).

Support Provided

If difficulties are encountered, what sort of support is provided? Is help given quickly and as unobtrusively as possible? With some children frustration is not easily tolerated, and a stage in learning is rapidly reached at which 'can't do it' becomes 'won't do it'. Timely intervention by the teacher can prevent the development of this sort of confrontation. Early help during the practice phase of a lesson and branching group work are techniques which can be usefully deployed (Chapter 3).

Sometimes, if it is too blatant and obvious, the support system itself can become a source of contention. Children can react very strongly against what they may interpret as an attempt to make them look foolish. Where teachers are aware of a child's learning difficulties, but claim that attempts to provide easier work or extra help have been rejected or abused, it is worth discussing with them the problems associated with 'overcompensation' (Chapter 3).

Marking

How are marks given and recorded? Are these a source of consistent and sometimes public humiliation? Apart from driving instruction, adults rarely meet situations in which they are faced with persistently poor performance on their own part. Teachers, almost by definition, have seldom faced such situations during their own schooldays. It is not difficult, however, to appreciate how easy it is for pupils to transform the old adage and decide that 'if at first you don't succeed, give up and pretend you don't care'.

Particularly when poor marks result not from lack of effort in a specialist subject, but from presentational errors in writing and spelling, they can be a source of resentment. Sometimes publicising poor marks can result in silly, clownish behaviour, as a display of indifference, on the part of children who have done badly. Usually the response is a less direct, but growing disaffection with the subject and its teacher, which is at the root of problems which crop up at other times in the lesson.

Marking is essential for record keeping and providing feedback, so if success is not being achieved, some feeling of failure cannot be avoided. The ultimate answer might be in a radical restructuring of the curriculum so that steps in learning are so gradual that even slow learners can make error-free progress. This is obviously a long-term aim and more difficult to achieve in some subjects than in others. More immediately, discussion should focus on the possibilities of dual marks for skill and effort, concentrating on improving one aspect of presentation at a

time, and relating marks to personal performance instead of class competition (Chapter 3).

Rewards

The way in which marks are linked to rewards can be a crucial factor in
determining whether a child retains motivation or what Weber (1982)
terms 'momentum', even in a subject he finds difficult. What sort of
reward system is used? Do all pupils have a fair chance of gaining
rewards for industry, if not for excellence? Exclusion from whatever
system of reward is used can lead to a feeling that it is pointless even to
try. This may be accompanied by an affectation of disdain for rewards
which are offered and disparagement for those who do strive for them.

If reward consists of praise or relies on the intrinsic motivation of
interest in lesson content, then the contingent use of teacher attention
could be a starting point for discussion (Chapter 4). This could lead to an
exploration of whether some children do need some extrinsic and tangible rewards as a first step towards rebuilding self-esteem in an area in
which they are failing (Chapter 4).

It is not easy to 'rekindle the dying embers of academic fire'
(Hawisher and Calhoun, 1978) amongst 30 or more pupils, often of
very mixed ability. Rather than seek a radical restructuring of the
reward system, it is better at this stage to concentrate on ensuring
participation in the present structure.

If praise is deemed sufficient reward, then how can the problem
pupil gain his share of it? This may be managed by asking him easier
questions and giving him simpler tasks, though this should be done with
subtlety or it becomes too blatantly patronising (Chapter 3). If house
points or some other formal recognition is given, then a scale linking them
to defined targets of class work can ensure that all pupils hve a chance of
gaining some public recognition of their efforts (Chapter 4). If possible,
without drastically altering their structure, lessons might be rearranged
so that more favoured activities act as reinforcers for less favoured ones
(Chapter 4).

Minimum Intervention

Advice on changes should always aim at keeping interference with
normal routine to a minimum. Heron (1978) suggests that whenever one
teacher intervenes in the work of another, the principle of Occam's
razor should be applied. This requires that the 'most parsimonious'

intervention, hence the least disturbing intervention, should be implemented, and more drastic measures tried only if this is ineffective. In other words, try the simplest way first.

Thus far this chapter has been framed in terms of what might be called a case discussion between colleagues. In a sense, this talking about a problem at second hand with a colleague is the first and least disturbing line of intervention. Suggestions are made by the consultant teacher, based on confidence in the ability and competence of his colleague. Not all the points mentioned would be raised at one interview, but, taken together, they provide a framework for an informal advisory approach.

At a more formal level, senior teachers may perceive a need for more direct intervention. This might take the form of personal observation and guidance, through team teaching or additional in-service training. For young and inexperienced teachers, the best place to start might be with a reminder of basic techniques for classroom management (Chapter 1). Indeed, as a part of their induction to teaching all probationers should have some such course at school or local authority level. Similarly, staff seminars on ways of providing for children with special needs in the ordinary class could be another form of indirect intervention (Sewell, 1982).

In general, however, in-service training is a lengthy and long-term solution to problems that are immediate and urgent. In looking for methods of intervention that will produce speedy results with the least disruption and without loss of confidence or face in the class teacher's part, the consultant should start from the premise that it is simpler to change the behaviour of the pupil than that of the teacher.

Intervention with Individual Pupils

This might start by observation of the context in which learning takes place, then consideration of the content of material and, finally, the possibilities of conditioning behaviour.

Focus on the context would require an examination of the present 'learning environment'. It may well be easy for an experienced eye to spot changes which can accommodate difficulties by providing easier access to help, support or control. Seating arrangements might be revised to decrease distraction or increase contact with the teacher. Distribution of materials might be rearranged to avoid delays in starting work. Monitorial jobs might be reassigned in ways which provide useful social employment for potentially disruptive children (Chapter 1).

In teaching, more than most activities, it is true that the onlooker sees more of the game. The pressures of constant interaction make it difficult for a teacher to observe his own performance objectively. A third party may be able to give helpful guidance on mannerisms or inflections of the voice, which appear to signal unintended belligerence or unnecessary insecurity. However, the presence of a third party is also likely to change the behaviour of all participants in a lesson. With a senior colleague present, a teacher is likely to be unduly nervous and a class may be uncharacteristically constrained.

Focus on content should concentrate on identifying and reducing difficulties caused by inability to cope with material which may be too demanding. The presence of a second teacher should increase the opportunity to talk through problems with pupils, identifying which concepts are proving difficult to understand and which texts are difficult to comprehend.

Providing some immediate relief from pressure may be the senior teacher's main intention at this stage, but he cannot remain as a sort of permanent co-pilot. It is vital therefore that discussion of content should be based on a series of questions that can continue to be used as a form of self-evaluation, assessing difficulty, variety, alternatives, revision and questions strategies (Chapter 2).

If changes in context and content fail to improve the situation, then the principles of conditioning may need to be applied to developing a programme of behaviour modification. This may be necessary because of the intransigence of a particular child. In this case, the presence of an observer can be a great help for the establishment of a 'baseline', deciding what are really effective rewards or suitable behavioural goals for a 'contract' or determining an appropriate rate of exchange as part of a 'token economy' (Chapter 4). As a last resort, it may be necessary to confirm that punishment needs to be used to deter seriously disruptive activities. The senior teacher is likely to have access to a more effective range of sanctions in this respect. However, before this stage is reached, it may well be appropriate to look at ways in which class behaviour can be changed.

Intervention with a Class

The peer group may frequently encourage problem behaviour by its conscious or unconscious reaction to the individual concerned. Often, it is more effective and easier to alter that response than to attempt to suppress the original behaviour by punishment. The approval or amusement of contemporaries is such a potent reinforcer that it can outweigh all but the harshest of punishments (Chapter 4).

Advice should be aimed at suggesting how the teacher might involve the group in helping the individual. Direct discussion with a class could be used to illustrate the benefits of making their attention contingent on sensible rather than silly behaviour. This may be linked with seating rearrangements in which the potential disrupter is brought to the front, so that others are no longer tempted to turn round to look at him. It could also be used as an explanation of why one individual is singled out for 'Contracting' to perform a behaviour which others do without reward. Teachers often worry about this apparently preferential treatment of wrongdoers. Other pupils do not usually complain about this being unfair, and indeed being taken into the teacher's confidence in this way may be sufficient reward in itself.

Direct discussion can also be the best way to launch a token economy. Not only does this allow children to participate in deciding what should be suitable rewards, but it should also help avoid the negative and uncooperative responses which might greet an imposed system. If a token or points system becomes a source of argument, it may be fatally undermined. This is less likely to happen if the class is involved in its inception. One or two recalcitrant individuals can be easily drawn in once everybody else is committed to enjoying the game (Chapter 4).

Some teachers, particularly if they lack confidence in their dealings with the class as a whole, may prefer a more indirect approach to involving the group in helping the individual. They may use praise, tokens or more tangible rewards to encourage fellow pupils to ignore provocative remarks and irresponsible actions on the part of children who seem intent on disrupting lessons.

Another useful idea is the recruitment of a more competent and mature classmate as a peer tutor or teaching aide to help with overcoming difficulties in work and to show a better example in behaviour.

Intervention with Teachers

There are times when it will become evident that problems lie not so much with the children themselves as with their teacher's lack of understanding, inappropriate expectations or inadequate training. One possible response is to provide a good model of academic and social management — either from the consultant teacher or other teachers becoming involved in team teaching. Though difficult to arrange in response to a crisis, this approach might be seen as more of a preventive measure, with some portion of every probationer teachers' timetable being given to team teaching with more experienced colleagues.

Where troubles arise in relation to one or two pupils, consideration might be given to their withdrawal from certain lessons. This is often done in the guise of providing remedial help, though unless some specific learning difficulty has been diagnosed, this may be a misuse of that service. In other schools there may be a special unit or a teacher with a designated responsibility for looking after children excluded from particular lessons. Although this provides some immediate relief, withdrawal can rarely be a long-term solution. It does not in itself help the teacher to develop more effective techniques.

Another form of support, which is helpful when there is particular antagonism between a pupil and teacher, is providing backup by requiring the child to report after each lesson to a senior teacher. This might be seen as simply another form of punishment, but it can also be used to provide counselling and feedback to both parties. This gives the more experienced teacher the chance to check whether his colleague's expectations are realistic and to amend them, diplomatically of course, through discussion of the child's work and behaviour.

As mentioned previously, more formal in-service training programmes will also have a part to play. Either within the school itself or perhaps more effectively through the local authority advisory service, courses should be mounted which give teachers the opportunity to explore and discuss the wealth of literature and experience of effective classroom management.

6 TEACHER STRESS

All teachers are aware that teaching gives rise to stress, which Kyriacou (1980) has described as: 'The experience of a whole range and mixture of unpleasant emotions, predominantly tension, with anxiety, depression and a feeling of being emotionally drained.' When considering a teacher's management of children, it is useful to remember that experience of disruptive pupils not only gives rise to stress during and after any incident of disruption in a classroom, but the stress itself affects the teacher's behaviour in ways that make disruptive behaviour more probable. When children continually frustrate a teacher, he feels irritated and, if the frustration continues, the irritation leads to anger. As Dohrenwend (1961) has pointed out, it can be 'anger in', that is, directed towards the self, or 'anger out', directed towards other people or objects in the environment. For a teacher's performance, and for the effects of anger on children, the direction that the anger takes is important. If the direction is 'in', then the teacher has to cope with the effects of this anger directed towards himself. If it is 'out', then he has to manage the effects of his anger directed towards the children, one of these effects being that his angry behaviour may stimulate angry responses in children, increasing the probability of disruption and possible confrontation.

It seems that in their initial training, although they hear about the emotions of children, teachers do not have the opportunity to understand the effects of children's behaviour upon them. They are given little guidance as to how they are to cope with their feelings of irritation, frustration or anger. How they manage these feelings has a direct bearing on their classroom management. It does not help teachers looking for guidance to deny that anger follows continual frustration, or the children's exposure of their lack of skills in the management of them. Although standards of professional conduct can prevent teachers from expressing or acting out their feelings in classrooms, these standards are not quickly gained. Furthermore, acceptance of the importance of having these standards may go some way in preventing teachers from acting out their angry feelings (although frank discussions in staff rooms reveal that anger, in the face of gross provocation, slips past the professional censor), but the code of professional conduct does not prevent anger from arising. Classroom experience enables teachers to put together a repertoire of management skills which helps them to avoid situations that would provoke their anger, and to find ways of showing their anger that do not trigger off further hostility as they deal with provocative behaviour. In doing this, they make their anger innocuous, although it is not ineffective. There is an important difference in the attitude of a provocative child to an angry teacher who denigrates him, who makes sarcastic or wounding comments, and one whose demeanour shows that she is angry, and may say that she is, but who expresses her anger in reasonable terms. It is helpful for teachers to recognise that the behaviour of some children will make them angry, and that a denial that this is so, or denial that they feel anger, will not help them to bring anger under control. They are more likely to do this if they reflect on the events that led to the sequence of events that first frustrated them, then irritated them, and finally made them angry. The importance of this reflection and rumination is considered in greater depth later in the chapter.

Dunham (1976), like Kyriacou, also identifies anxiety as a response to stress commenting that anxiety is 'associated with feelings of inadequacy, loss of confidence confusion of thinking and occasionally, panic'. When an unpleasant incident between a teacher and a child in a classroom is looked at closely, then the teacher's feeling of anxiety, with the accompanying feelings of inadequacy, loss of confidence, the panic that leads to recognisable confusion in thinking and acting, becomes plain. It is therefore worth while to look rather more closely at teacher anxiety and its effects upon children, because this anxiety is frequently a cause of disruptive behaviour in classrooms. The adage 'Quiet teacher, quiet class' was mentioned in Chapter 1. We may add 'Anxious teacher — anxious children — disruptive incidents', although it is better to refer to 'very anxious teacher' so that he or she is distinguished from thousands of teachers who feel some anxiety about their performance and the children's responses to them, but whose behaviour does not betray their anxiety. Very anxious teachers communicate their anxiety to children, making them anxious in their turn. This leads to the consideration of what it is that very anxious teachers do or do not do in classrooms which shows their anxiety, and what it is that children do or do not do as a result of the teacher's behaviour.

Teachers' anxiety is communicated to the children in many ways, through their speech, their movements, through the ways in which they organise and present lesson material and activities, and through their reactions to children who may upset their management of their class, or who appear to upset it.

Communicating Anxiety through Speech

Very anxious teachers tend to give instructions in tentative or hesi
tant tones. This may be because they have not thought out clearly wha
it is that they want the children to do, but it may also be — and it ver
often is — because they anticipate some resistance or lack of co
operation. This hesitant manner has unfortunate results. It leads t
some confusion, because the children are not certain what it is tha
they have been asked to do. It gives the impression that the teache
may not know either. It also conveys to the children the impressior
first, that the teacher is not likely to insist on them doing somethin
that does not, on the sound of it, seem very convincing to him and
secondly, that he is not quite sure what he will do, if they do not obe
or co-operate.

Very anxious teachers are also likely to give a rapid stream o
instructions or requests without allowing children time to comply wit
one before they are overtaken by another. This leads to confusion, an
their conclusion that the teacher does not know what she is doin
These rapidly delivered instructions or orders sometimes include thos
that cannot be carried out because they are contradictory. It is no
unusual, ridiculous as it may seem, to hear a very anxious teacher us
such phrases as 'Now sit still and take your books out' or 'Stand sti
and move quietly'. These phrases convey to children the undoubte
fact that the teacher is confused. They are also likely to make request
of children, or to issue instructions that cannot be heard because the
speak when the general clatter in the classroom prevents the childre
from hearing. Such teachers are also likely to talk far too much, s
that children are irritated by the continual noise, and confused by th
variety of exhortations or criticisms. When listening to very anxiou
teachers, it seems that they are uneasy if there are noticeable perioc
of quiet in the room. They do not leave the children alone, their speec
is hurried, and they rarely speak in relaxed or reassuring tones.

Communicating Anxiety through Movement

In talking to a young teacher and hearing her describe the effectiv
ness with which the head of the school tackled any disruptive behaviou
she told how impressed she was by the way the headmaster walked. 'H
never runs, or seems to be in a hurry. He comes along with th
measured tread, as if there were all the time in the world.' The head

measured tread was not the only reason for his effectiveness, but the teacher had pointed to an important aspect of his interaction with children. The tread gave them the impression of the head's confidence and self-control.

This communication of self-control is an important feature of effective classroom management. One of the impressive characteristics of teachers who manage difficult situations successfully is the confidence that they give to children, who perceive that they are in control of themselves. It may be that in difficult situations a teacher cannot see more than one step ahead, but this uncertainty does not communicate to the class. They show this self-control in their movements and actions. They do not run about, or wave their arms around, or hurry here and there. One teacher described the anxious behaviour of a colleague, and its effect on him, very accurately when he said: 'Here he comes, running along the ceiling'. Observation of very anxious teachers shows that their movements indicate tension and restlessness, which communicate to the children and unsettle them. They hurry about, they use exaggerated movements too frequently, they always appear to be in a hurry. They knock into furniture and children, they drop things, and even when they are in one place, such as at their desk, they tend to shuffle papers or books about. The too talkative teacher seems to be the centre of unsettling noise; the overactive teacher is the centre of unsettling movement and disturbance.

Communicating Anxiety through Muddled Lesson Organisation

Very anxious teachers show their anxiety in the ways that confusion and indecisiveness characterise the presentation of lesson materials and activities. We saw in Chapter 1 the importance of the teacher's organisation of lesson activities in an ordered sequence that unfolds under his direction. When there is high anxiety present in teachers, this shows in the ways that they change their minds about what the children are to do and the sequence in which they are to do it; the way in which they start one activity and then leave it because they realise that they have left out some essential antecedent to it; the frequency with which they change their minds in asking children to carry out tasks, the number of times their lessons have to end hurriedly and in confusion because they have not timed their lessons correctly; the frequency with which they run out of lesson material before the bell goes, leaving them with an awkward interregnum. This gives children the impression that they are disorganised, which indeed they are. This disorganisation may be described as incompetence, but behind displays of incompetence there is often anxiety, which inhibits or prevents effective functioning. In describing the effects of heightened anxiety in teachers, Lindgen (1960) has commented that it narrows their perceptions, inhibits their ingenuity and reduces their ability to alter their techniques and methods. Hebb (1972) has also commented on the ways that anxiety impairs the ability to make decisions and results in confusion of thinking and action.

Communicating Anxiety in Interaction with Children

Children describe over-anxious teachers as being 'jumpy'. Their tension prompts them to jump quickly on behaviour which they *perceive* as being likely to interfere with their lessons, whether this behaviour is likely to or not. They do not intervene in the effective ways that Robertson (1981) has described, which show the children that the teacher is in command. Their interventions, accompanied by criticism or exhortations in impatient tones, give the impression that they are nearing the end of their resources and not at the beginning of them. They do not have the confidence to recognise which behaviour they might ignore, which would not continue anyway, and which calls for immediate intervention. It is often their reaction to the behaviour that prevents its disappearance, and their exclamations that magnify some minor incident to a major one. As Rutter and his co-authors have pointed out, successful learning and acceptable behaviour is more probable in classrooms where teachers make as few disciplinary interventions as possible (Rutter *et al.*, 1979).

As anxiety is circular in its effects, by behaving as they do, very anxious teachers affect children's behaviour negatively. If they are noisy the children tend to be noisy. If they are restless and over-active, the children are likely to be restless, and restless and noisy children are not far from being disruptive. But the effects of teachers' anxiety go further than this. They make children uneasy, because they sense their tension. The children who are most likely to be disruptive have quite probably a good deal of anxiety of their own. We know that many children with problems of adjustment are more anxious than children who do not have these problems. Children who have difficulties in coping with their own anxiety, without giving way to unacceptable behaviour, find it particularly difficult to cope with the anxiety of others. What they need is the reassuring presence of a teacher who shows that he can control them. What they perceive in the teacher who is noisy, jumpy, restless and disorganised is someone who cannot control himself and who is therefore not very likely to be able to control them. As their anxiety rises, they act out their feelings of unease in disruptive behaviour. In the face of this, the teacher becomes more and more anxious, and the negative circle is complete. Over-anxious teachers bring on just the behaviour that they do not want and are least able to manage. They present the children with poor models of behaviour. Thus whatever steps teachers can take to reduce their levels of anxiety benefit them not only by increasing their own comfort, but also by increasing their effectiveness.

Reducing Teacher Anxiety

Although there are many causes of stress in teachers, one of the principal causes is anxiety about their management of children, especially children who disrupt their lessons (Dunham, 1976; Kyriacou and Sutcliffe, 1977; Kyriacou, 1980). In talking to teachers about their anxieties arising from difficulties in the management of children, it seems that they worry that, if they cannot establish control quickly, disorder will spread quickly through the classroom and cause them increasing difficulties, and that they will lose the children's respect and the respect of their colleagues. To this may be added their concern that, as they are responsible for the children's standards of behaviour and the progress of their learning, their lack of control is an unsatisfactory response to the responsibilities that are entrusted to them. Teachers are conscientious. They have to discharge important tasks in handing on the values of the society in which they work — sometimes in circumstances where they feel they have not the support of those who might be their allies — so that the stress accompanying poor performance in the classroom is compounded by their feelings of disappointment with themselves. Taken altogether, this is a formidable weight of anxiety. Unless they can find ways of lessening it, they are unlikely to be able to function effectively.

This section is not concerned with ways that teachers can improve their management skills; these are considered in other sections of the book. It is concerned with suggestions as to how teachers might reduce their anxieties that surround difficulties encountered in classroom management, thus decreasing the probabilities of disruptive behaviour.

Kyriacou (1980) has shown that teachers reduce their anxieties in several ways. Teachers in a comprehensive school reported on strategies that they employed to reduce their anxiety. Among these were the following:

taking some immediate action on the basis of their understanding of the situation;

thinking objectively about the situations that caused them concern and keeping their feelings under control;

not letting the problem go until they had found some solution to it considering a range of plans for managing the source of their stress and setting these in some order or priority;

expressing their feelings of frustration to others so that they could think rationally about the problem;

talking of the stressful situations to colleagues at work.

Whatever strategies teachers employ to reduce their stresses, for any single strategy to be effective, the source of anxiety should be looked at as dispassionately and as honestly as possible. Thus, if a teacher adopts one of the most effective ways of reducing anxiety, which is to talk about it to someone else, she will derive most benefit from such an experience, if she is frank about her own behaviour in any disruptive incident in a classroom (if that is the source of anxiety) and open about her feelings of frustration — not only with the child concerned, but also about her disappointment and frustration with herself. It is not easy for some teachers to do this, and it can only be done with confidence if the teacher feels she can talk freely to someone who will not regard what she describes as an admission of incompetence. In this situation the listener gives help in two ways. He acts as a sounding board so that the other teacher finds her own ideas become clearer. It is a common experience when talking of problems to a good listener for us to exclaim: 'Well, I see now what I did wrong', before the listener has made any comment at all, except to encourage us to talk freely. The other help the good listener gives is the advice that he is able to offer.

Another way for a teacher to reduce stress arising from anxiety is for him to think very clearly about whatever incident or incidents cause the anxiety. In doing this, it is helpful to review the incident as if there were a listener present who needs to know the situation as exactly as possible. The facts to be clear about are listed below.

What did the child, or the children, actually do?

What did I do?

What happened just before the child did what she did, which was so disruptive?

What was I doing at the time?

How did the class react to the child's behaviour?

How did I react to what she did, or said?

How did I manage the behaviour (or behaviour similar to it), when it happened before?

Was it the particular child who aroused such indignation in me, and if so, what is it about him or her that I find hard to bear?

Have I ever done anything positive for the child?

If he or she has ever shown positiveness towards me, how have I reacted?

The benefits of sharing the problems of management with another person, or of proceeding with a self-examination such as the one suggested, are twofold. First of all, facing up to a source of anxiety and steeling oneself to look at it closely is beneficial, because it stops self-deception and denial of the reality of a situation. Whatever else teachers need to increase their effective management of children, they certainly need as much clarity in their thinking and acting as possible, and as little confusion as possible. Sometimes their feelings of regret or shame at their response to an unpleasant classroom incident leads teachers to thrust aside the recollection of the event. This is understandable, but not very helpful in reducing anxiety through tracking it to its source. Secondly, when a teacher reflects on children's behaviour in a classroom, and her reactions to it, or when she describes these to someone else, she frequently finds the clues she needs that will suggest how future problems may be overcome or avoided. These clues are somewhere in the actual transactions themselves, but during an encounter with a disruptive child or children, because of the rapidity of the events, because of the narrowing of perceptions which so often accompanies stressful situations, these clues are overlooked. This is borne out in many staff-room conversations that follow unpleasant incidents in a classroom. Teachers are heard to use such phrases as: 'If only I had realised that . . . ' 'If only I had noticed . . . ' 'If only I had stopped to see . . . '

Although he was primarily concerned with teachers' needs to find solutions to problems of behaviour rather than with their need to reduce their anxiety, Roberts (1977) has developed a technique — 'staff problem-solving groups'— which is effective in the reduction of teachers' anxieties arising from the management of children. He suggests that a group of teachers most frequently in contact with a child first agree upon some particular behaviour which presents them with the most difficulty. They then agree upon some strategy to reduce the frequency of this behaviour, discuss its appropriateness, put the strategy into action, and assess its effectiveness. This shared under-standing and agreed action is effective in reducing teachers' anxiety arising from children's disruptive behaviour. The group is supportive because individual descriptions and suggestions are valued, and because the proposed solututions arise from frank discussions about difficulties that all the teachers encounter. This frees a teacher from the demoralising belief that he is alone in having difficulties in managing a child. It reminds him that solutions to problems may be found when they are looked at carefully and honestly.

It is worth while to look at another strand that makes up the anxiety that teachers feel about their control of children — that the children will lose respect for them, if they do not show that they can control them. It would be foolish to deny that children have respect for teachers who manage them successfully. Robertson has described with great clarity the need for teachers to show their authority and effec-tiveness very early on in their encounters with children (Robertson, 1981), and he points to what is undoubtedly true. It is also true, however, that children's respect for teachers does not entirely depend upon their success in controlling them. Galwey (1970) and Harré and Rosser (1975) have provided some interesting evidence about teachers whom children respect. In talking to groups of secondary-school children, these authors found that they certainly respected teachers who could control them, but they commented that they also respected teachers who:

> did not bore them — in the children's eyes, good discipline went with interest and achievement;
> were not very strict disciplinarians;
> did not put on acts, but were themselves;
> could express genuine anger, when this was appropriate;
> did not waste time in insisting on unreal standards of quietness and conformity;
> did not shout at them and were not rude to them;
> did not have favourites;
> were conscientious in setting and marking homework;
> did not attempt to be as friendly in class as they were in social situa-tions away from the classroom;

were humourous;

could admit that they were wrong;

were not prepared to see school rules broken with impunity, but did not make an inordinate fuss about such infractions as did occur;

continually involved children in the activities and learning experiences in their lessons;

showed that they were concerned that the children went to their lessons;

did not 'treat us like kids',

showed their concern by taking the trouble to find out children's names;

were fair and treated them as individuals.

For teachers who worry that their difficulties in controlling children will mean that they will lose their respect for them, these views on teachers should be reassuring. If a teacher is conscientious, courteous to children and colleagues, prepares and presents interesting lessons, is fair and avoids sarcasm, is not pompous, nor petty, children will respect him. Furthermore, such a teacher will find that his positive attitudes towards children and his behaviour in the classroom go a long way to prevent problems of management from arising in the first place. The confidence that comes from knowledge of classroom management techniques will prove helpful, but techniques on their own are not sufficient for successful teaching. This calls for techniques which are grounded in positive attitudes towards children.

Anxiety that their colleagues will think them incompetent if they cannot manage children is a potent cause of stress among teachers who have not had enough experience to develop their strategies for managing children successfully. The difficulty is that teachers' failures are public failures, and public to children whom they particularly want to impress. And, as if this were not unpleasant enough, the comparison of their failure with their colleagues' successes is also public – they are well aware that the children make these comparisons. There are few more wounding comments to teachers than: 'It's not like this when Mr Best takes us, sir. He [the boy causing the trouble] wouldn't dare to muck about like that.' In the same way, there are few more confounding experiences for a teacher who, having had a rough passage with a class, goes ito the staffroom and says: 'Oh dear! I have just had a frightful time with 4Z' and hears an experienced member of staff say: '4Z? What, 4Z – they never give *me* any trouble.'

In finding ways of allaying the anxiety about what their colleagues think of his performance, it is better for a teacher to swallow his pride and ask for help, before he runs into deeper water. In some schools such help is provided, because it is a recognised feature of staff training and development, but this is not so in all schools.

It is better if the teacher who seeks advice from an experienced and skilled colleague describes his difficulties as precisely as possible, and focuses on one problem at a time, beginning with the one that causes the most trouble. It is not easy for a colleague to give help, if problems of management are presented to her in general terms. There is a good deal of difference between the request: 'Will you give me some tips about controlling 4Z?' and: 'Can you tell me how I can prevent children from rushing towards the door when the bell rings?' or 'What can I do if Jenkins makes the class laugh when I ask him a question?' Such questions make it easier to open a dialogue about specific items of behaviour so that the colleague can point to specific solutions.

Where it is acceptable, an inexperienced teacher can find a great deal of help from observing skilled colleagues at work in their classrooms. It is here that he can observe the management strategies that a colleague uses to ensure that the lesson proceeds smoothly. In their initial training, teachers have periods of observation in schools, but for the teacher seeking help in classroom management, the more useful observation is deliberately focused on interchanges between teacher and children. The observer pays close attention to the ways in which the more experienced colleague either avoids difficult situations or manages those that arise. There is a temptation for inexperienced teachers to believe that effective teachers owe their success to their charismatic qualities. It is true that some teachers have gifts of temperament and character in more abundance than others but if such teachers are observed closely, it is possible to recognise skills that they deploy. Although their gifts of personality are their own, it is possible for an onlooker who knows what he is looking for to identify skills that he may adapt to his own use. No one can wear somebody else's clothes, but there are some garments that will fit the borrower reasonably well! Marland (1975) has drawn attention to the craft of teaching and he is right to do so. Teaching *is* a craft, and a craft that takes a good deal of learning. All learners make mistakes — indeed, the mistakes are valuable aspects of the learning. As effective teachers are craftsmen, it is worth while to remember that craftsmen respect their materials. They do not abuse them. They find ways of working with recalcitrant and resistant materials. The more they work with them, the more they appreciate their possibilities. If teachers respect children, many problems of management diminish, some disappear, and all fall into better perspective. Respecting children — which does not mean allowing them to do as they please — prevents teachers from making those mistakes which are likely to stir up hostility and resentment, which, in turn, increase the probability of disruptive behaviour.

7 IMPERTURBABLE, RESILIENT AND IRRITATING TEACHERS

This chapter is concerned with observations of the classroom management of teachers, describing what they actually did or did not do which prevented disruptive behaviour, or extinguished it quickly when it did occur, or elicited hostile and resentful behaviour in children, which increased the probability of disruption. From his study of the interactions of teachers with children in a comprehensive school, and from his discussion with children and staff, Jordan (1974) concluded that some teachers could be described as 'deviance insulative'. These teachers:

> assumed that children wished to work, and if they did not work they could provide conditions in classrooms which would motivate them to work;
> had clear rules and made them explicit;
> were firm;
> did not have favourites;
> avoided confrontations;
> rarely made negative evaluative comments on deviant children (or children they perceived as deviant);
> when they punished children, allowed them opportunities to 'save face';
> did not denigrate children publicly in classrooms or privately to colleagues;
> were optimistic, assuming that all children would behave and co-operate;
> perceived all children as potential contributors to class activities; did not assume that deviant chilren were unlikely to alter their behaviour;
> liked and respected all children;
> cared about deviants and told them they did;
> were good-humoured and trusting,
> enjoyed meeting children outside the classroom.

This list is more helpful in its description of the attitudes of 'deviant-insulative' teachers towards children than in its descriptions of what such teachers actually did in their classrooms. For teachers without much experience of classroom management it is the question of what successful teachers do or do not do which is so important to them, and such descriptions are given at a later stage in the chapter. But before considering that, it is worth while to emphasise that teachers' positive attitudes towards children are fundamentally important as the ***groundwork on which effective techniques are based.*** A teacher without these attitudes can get along well enough for a time, and some do, but in the long run effective techniques of management alone are not enough. With effective and successful teachers, their management techniques are so much part of their teaching style and fit this style so well, that it is difficult to disentangle attitudes from techniques. It is not impossible, however, as the description of the mathematics teacher and the craft teacher which are included here, shows; both of them would fit into Jordan's 'deviance-insulative' category. The maths teacher, when observed, impressed one as a teacher whose management was so effective that it did not seem to cross any child's mind that he would not co-operate in the maths lesson or attempt to disrupt it. The craft teacher was somewhat different. Her management was not so embracing nor as complete, but she never let any disruptive behaviour spread from its point of origin to other children.

The Imperturbable Teacher

Whenever possible, and he made it possible on a surprising number of occasions, the maths teacher was in the classroom before the children whom he was to teach arrived. If there were other children in the room who had not left it to go to other classes, he usually ignored them. He then cleaned the chalkboard if this was necessary, and sat down. In many lessons he did not get up again until he left the room, although he did sometimes walk quietly around the class. This quietness was a noticeable feature of his behaviour. He very rarely raised his voice and rarely made any gestures whatever, except to point to the board if he had written or drawn on it.

When the children came into the room they sat down, as they knew that the first half of the lesson was the oral part, when he taught them some new material or took up some unfinished explanations of the previous lesson. In doing this, he asked the children to comment on what he had told them, he asked questions as necessary and put these questions to all the children in the room. It was noticeable that he spoke to the class as if every member of it had something to contribute to what-every question he raised. If a child said something which was patently irrelevant or which showed he had not grasped a point, his reaction was interesting. He would look at the child with a mixture of concern and slight bewilderment, and then say: 'No, that cannot be right – you have not thought about that. Listen . . . ' and he would put in a few more clues for the child to grasp – he did not dismiss the contribution out of hand. If impatience from other children showed that the child was not able to grasp whatever he supposed was plain, his most summary response was: 'You don't understand. I will try and clear that up with you later on.' This was said without reproach and certainly without threat, and in the second part of the lesson he would make another attempt.

In the second part of the lesson the children did the work set, which was focused on the explanations of the first part. While they did this, he sat at his desk, asked the child who had shown confusion in the earlier part of the lesson to bring his book to the desk, and he then gave whatever help was appropriate. It was here that any child still in difficulties could approach him for any help that he needed with the work set. If children talked, he asked them what was the matter and waited for an explanation. If it satisfied him, he made some comment that made it clear that they should get on with their work. If it did not, he looked at the offender for an appreciable period. This steady gaze was a feature of his behaviour that the children commented on. Sometimes nothing followed, as it was sufficient to overawe the offender. But sometimes something did – a sharp reprimand given in that quiet tone already mentioned, which was neither challenging nor hostile. Sometimes this was accompanied by a bit of 'stage business'. He took out a small notebook and, apparently, wrote the child's name in it. There was no direct evidence that every offender's name was in the book. But there was evidence, as any persistent offender discovered later on, if he had too frequently exceeded the limits that were set on behaviour, that all the occasions when he had offended were on record, and restitution was sought. This took the form of a detention, in which work was set and marked before the child went home. Why some child's name was thus recorded and retrieved and others were not seemed a mystery to most of his classes, but it was not. He knew the individuals in each class very well and knew for which children the detention was an appropriate punishment and which of them would be sufficiently warned by the entry in his book. As the children commented: 'You never knew when he had got you – it was best not to risk it.'

It was also during the second part of each lesson that he turned to the homework books on his desk. On the top of this was a card with the name of any child whose homework book was not included. He would say: 'Jenkins, I do not seem to have your homework. Why is that?' This was in the tone of question put to discover information and it was not put in a challenging or threatening tone. 'I do not seem to have . . . ' implied that he might have made some mistake in his collection and marking of the books. Jenkins's explanation was followed by a request that he should give in the work by a certain time, or by the appearance of the notebook. Whichever way he accepted or rejected the explanation, the work was inevitably done.

Below the cards with any names of children who had not given in their homework were the books of children whose work showed that they needed some help. This he provided as far as he could in the time available. The books at the bottom of the pile belonged to those whose work was successfully done. When handing them their books, he made some positive and encouraging remarks to them.

In the last few minutes of the lesson, and before the bell rang, he asked the children to stop work and pass their books forward. His last act was to pick up the pile of books, clean the board if he had either written or drawn on it, and sit down at the desk. After the bell rang, he told the children to go to their next lesson and, as was not surprising, he knew what this was. He then left the room with them.

The children, in the third, fourth and fifth years of a comprehensive school, enjoyed these lessons. They commented that he was fair and decent, that he treated them as individuals. They thought he was a bit hard, commenting: 'You cannot get away with it – he knows.' But they also remarked that he made them work hard and they learned a good deal. One of the noticeable features of his lessons was the amount of work both he and the classes got through. He did not waste their time, and they certainly did not waste his. In the classroom, there was a perceptible air of confidence and industriousness. The classroom routine was predictable – he was predictable. Unsettling classroom events, on the whole, did not happen. If maths apparatus had to be given out, there were monitors to do this. Only on very rare occasions did he turn his back on the class to look into a cupboard or go into a store room. When he did do this, there was usually some increase in the amount of noise, which on his return he usually ignored. But again, the children could not count on this, because sometimes he would make a comment about the misfortune of some children who could not be trusted to work unless someone stood over them. At other times, he consulted his notebook.

In considering the effectiveness of the maths teacher, we recognise that there were several positive features in his situation. He was a maths specialist teaching a subject he liked to the top two streams of older children. He did not have to manage in a class situation where children needed to move about using apparatus or equipment, which would give opportunities for children to play about. He had an equitable temperament. But when allowance is made for these circumstances, the fact remains that he behaved towards children in the way that Jordan suggests that 'deviance-insulative' teachers behave, and that he was the kind of teacher whom children reported to Harré and Rosser and to Galwey that they respected. What was it that he did or did not do to deserve this respect?

First, he respected the children. He showed this in the way that he spoke to them, in the way that he listened to them. He did not shout at them, or assume that they were in the wrong until he had established this — as was shown in his question to the boy about his homework. When he had to reprimand a child, he did this in even tones and in the same manner as his ordinary speech. O'Leary and others (1977) have reported on a research study showing that quiet reprimands privately delivered are more effective than public ones loudly proclaimed. He assumed that all the children in the class were able to understand the lesson topic and included all of them in the questions he asked. If they could not answer, he showed patience and willingness to give further information.

His respect was also shown in the work that he set. He knew it would make demands on their abilities. The children thought he was a little too demanding at times, but in making the demands he demonstrated the undoubted fact that appropriate demands are supportive. The care with which he set and marked homework also showed his respect for the children; he expected them to do it, and they expected him to show his interest in what they did by marking it.

Second, he prepared the lessons carefully. This preparation extended to small details. The monitors to whom the books were passed sat at the front of each row of desks. It took him some time putting the homework books in the order he wanted. The books belonging to the children he wanted to talk to were always at the top of the pile, so he lost no time in shuffling through a pile of books looking for the one he wanted. He learned and remembered all the children's names. He knew their timetables, so that he knew to which lesson they went after his. All this took him a considerable time, but the effect of it all emphasised that he always had the intitiative — he did not have to rely on children to prompt him. His timing contributed to his preservation of the initiative. He was not overtaken by the end of the lesson, he was ready for it.

Third, his demeanour in the classroom — his quiet voice and quiet movement around the clsss — emphasised that he was in control of himself. More than that, his classroom behaviour and his own industriousness acted as cues to the behaviour and the performance that he wanted. What he did was in line with what he expected the children to do. He had his idea of the learning environment that he wanted and he preserved this. Any marked deviation from it was noticeable and exceptional.

Fourth, he did not give chances for disruptive behaviour to begin. He was in the classroom before the children arrived, whenever this was possible. He did not leave the class with his back to them to rummage in cupboards — it is hardly surprising that the cupboards in the maths room were in apple-pie order so he knew where he could lay his hands on what he needed very quickly.

Finally, although he did not appear to know that he did, he made use of a very effective behavioural technique. As the children perceived this, they were not sure 'When he had got you — it's better not to risk it.' They referred to his use of his notebook. What he was doing was to use intermittent negative reinforcement on a variable ratio. Children are negatively reinforced if they do something to avoid an unpleasant or adversive experience. If, for example, children will only work to avoid being nagged, to avoid this they do their work — they have been negatively reinforced (Vargas, 1977). If negative reinforcement is intermittent, they do not know when to expect an unpleasant experience so they work or behave all the time, because they do not know when the unpleasant experience will overtake them. If the negative reinforcement is not on a regular basis but it varies, then the uncertainty is increased and their avoidance of the unpleasant consequences is continuous. He used other well-known behavioural techniques. He ignored unacceptable behaviour which he decided was trivial. He rewarded the behaviour and the performance that he wanted.

Because he had little humour, because of his punctiliousness and his rather unremitting commitment to high standards, he was not the most popular member of staff. The children liked him, however. He was what Meighan (1978) has described as a 'nice strict teacher'. The older children, who had a shrewd appreciation of the differences between effective and ineffective teachers, expressed their gratitude to him for the habits of work he instilled in them. One made an interesting comment: 'Old T never shopped you — he dealt with you himself'.

The Resilient Teacher

There were noticeable differences between the craft teacher and the maths teacher previously described. It was more obvious that the craft teacher enjoyed working with children; she was less meticulous and less restrained. She was more humorous and more outgoing. She relied less on non-verbal communication. Whereas the maths teacher reacted to any unwanted behaviour with a look of surprise and slight disdain, she would use such phrases as 'Oh, come on – don't be a silly ass'. She tended to be critical of children, but she did not denigrate them in public. When she thought it appropriate to 'sort Mary out', she did this privately when no other children were present. She was enthusiastic about art and craft, and this enthusiasm spread to the children. Because the children were free to talk and move about during her lessons, she had to manage in a less structured situation than the maths teacher. There were more opportunities for children to mess about and waste time. She had made the rules clear that regulated their use of the art and craft apparatus, and frequently stopped the work of the class to remind them of these. It was noticeable that the children accomplished a great deal in her lessons and that as she moved quietly around the class she was on hand to encourage them. When she did criticise children's work, she always prefaced the criticism by drawing attention to whatever positive features there were in it. She made more frequent use of praise than the maths teacher, whose expectation of good work was one of the criticisms expressed about him.

Her control of the class was not as embracing as her colleague's. The atmosphere in the craft room was more relaxed than the atmosphere in the maths room, and there were usually one or two children who did not work consistently or who made more noise than she thought appropriate. It was noticeable that this noise or time-wasting did not spread to other children. In insulating it, it was interesting to note that she knew how to respond to the child concerned – her reactions to unwanted behaviour were on a graduate scale. With some children, she brought them back to their task with remarks expressed in conversational tones. If this was not sufficient, there was a noticeable acerbity in what she said. The criticisms were not expressed as a threat, nor as a challenge, but they were pointed. With other children, she did not use a conversational tone as a preface to the more critical remarks. Her comments began at a sharper level, because she knew that they would respond better to that approach. With children whom she knew to be potential disrupters, she quashed any misbehaviour very quickly.

It was here that she came nearest to issuing ultimatums, but she did this carefully. She used phrases that made it clear there would be unpleasant consequences if she were not obeyed, but she avoided challenging children. What she said showed that the consequences of their misbehaviour were certain, but that, as they knew what they were, they could avoid them. This was conveyed in quiet tones — the tones, in fact, of someone reasoning with reasonable individuals. Her assumption that children would behave reasonably in response to reasonable treatment underlay much of her success in her classroom management.

Sometimes, of course, a child who was disrupting a class did not behave reasonably. When this happened, her response was swift. The child was told to clear up her craft materials and go to the head of house. This was a rare occurrence, a final action that she did not call on carelessly. It was an arrangement that she and the head of house had agreed. She had thought out the implications of having to seek help from a colleague and the effects of this on her classes. She was quite frank about it and, as she explained it, it was a reasonable thing to do. She said that she would not become involved in a confrontation that she knew she might not be able to manage, and that she was not going to be involved in an undignified and pointless verbal dispute with a child who would be sustained in the interchange by an audience. She emphasised that she did not shout at children nor nag them, but that she treated them with courtesy, and she expected them to treat her as she treated them. If they did not, she was defeated and it was no use to pretend otherwise. She said that if a child repeatedly defied her and would not give way, she could not make her, and she was not going to attempt to do it by using threats or abuse or by being drawn into a confrontation that might escalate, or become ridiculous. She did not think that calling on a senior colleague for help weakened her position in respect of the child she sent to the head of house or the other children in the class. She reported that when a child complained to her that she was unfair in referring her to the head of house, she said: 'What did you expect? You wanted me to argue with you and you hoped to make me rattled. You were really hoping to show off, and you wouldn't show off on your own with Miss W. You had the chance of avoiding trouble and you did not take it. You know I am not going to fight [she did not mean a physical fight] with anyone in the classroom. I have never been any different.'

Her reference to a senior colleague is worth exploring a little further. Teachers do not like doing this, because they have the reasonable anxiety that, if they have to call on a colleague for help, this undermines their authority. It is true, of course, that if the craft teacher did this frequently, her authority would be undermined, although it is more true to say that she would not have had much in the first place. It is no use for a teacher to attempt to *establish* authority by constant reliance on somebody else, but the craft teacher's position was different. Her own classroom management was secure. She had made it secure by her attitudes to the children and the skills she practised. Having done this, calling on a colleague was one of her resources that she would use when appropriate.

In their management of children in classes, teachers are expected to be continually successful. Such an assumption certainly is made, but it is interesting that it is not made about their ability to teach children who have difficulties in mastering the basic subjects, or who show real problems of adjustment. Most teachers have few inhibitions about declaring their inability to help backward readers, or those who are described as maladjusted. They do not feel threatened when they refer a child to a school counsellor or to a colleague whom they recognise as having particular skills in counselling. They have few inhibitions about seeking assistance from a remedial teacher for children with reading difficulties, or from an educational psychologist or a school counsellor for children they regard as maladjusted. But they are apt to feel differently about seeking assistance in classroom management, because they consider this a reflection on their own authority and professional competence. At the same time, in listening to teachers describing their training, it seems that they do not spend much time in lectures or demonstrations which focus on the problems of management. The idea that a well-prepared, well-presented imaginative lesson will prevent disruptive behaviour is very prevalent. This is undoubtedly true, but it is not true enough! As one teacher put it: 'No one ever told me what I should do when the chips went down in the geography lesson!'

Of course, the reliance on a colleague's help is a two-way transaction. The colleague outside the classroom, not knowing the events that lead to a call for assistance, cannot be expected to accept one side of the story only and behave to the child as if these antecedent events were of no importance. The disruptive child may disrupt a poor lesson with an ineffectual teacher who brings troubles down on her own head. The teacher who asks for assistance may be what Hargreaves has called a 'deviance-provocative teacher' — one who behaves in ways that are described later on in the chapter. There has to be confidence between the teacher who asks for assistance and the one providing it. It may be that the absent colleague will point to errors that the teacher made in her initial dispute with a child, and the teacher should be prepared to accept an assessment of the situation from one not caught up in the incident. If this is done in a judgemental manner, it is not likely to be very helpful. It calls for sensitivity and frankness. However distasteful it is for a teacher to ask for assistance, it is preferable to the consequences of becoming involved in the sort of confrontation described in Chapter 9.

When the craft teacher reminded the child that she had had the chance to avoid trouble, that she had not taken it, that it was known in the craft room that there was a point beyond which reference to the head of house was made, she demonstrated an important rule of effective management — the children knew what to expect if they persisted in disruption. Having made up her mind where her limits were, and being quite clear about the way in which she would operate in critical situations, the craft teacher stuck to her procedures. She also illustrated the point that Dreikurs (1968) makes. He suggests that as some children are set upon a power struggle with the teacher in order to gain recognition, this inappropriate way of gaining such recognition is best prevented by denying them the opportunity for it. In some circumstances this may be impossible, but, as with a confrontation, it is better if a teacher keeps the initiative in deciding whether it would serve any useful purpose.

In talking to the child who taxed her with her reference to the senior colleague, the craft teacher showed that she was prepared to talk seriously with a child about a serious matter. This was one of her characteristics that the children commented on — that although she would not argue publicly with them, they knew that she would listen to them, if they put their views to her privately. It underlined her respect for them. This was one of her strengths. Another was the plain demonstration that, as she treated the children fairly, she made no secret of the fact that she expected them to treat her the same way. She knew her own strength and did not attempt to go beyond it. This prevented her from becoming involved in confrontation which she could not win in public, because she was not prepared to give up her dignified stance in the face of provocation. She knew that a child determined to get the better of her would say or do things which were not compatible with the standards she set herself. In this, she set a good example of adult behaviour.

In some ways, the craft teacher illustrated the attitudes and skills of the 'deviance-insulative' teacher better than the maths teacher did. With him, class troubles did not seem to arise, at least as far as observation went. They may have done so when he first began teaching, but, if they did, it is reasonable to suppose that he developed and refined management techniques which he found effective and which he later showed to such advantage. In the craft teacher's lesson, it was possible to observe the beginnings of some unwanted behaviour which she insulated.

The Irritating Teacher

One difference between the geography teacher and the craft and the maths teachers was apparent at the beginning of his lessons. The children were not allowed to go straight into his classroom, even when no other class was in it. They had to line up in the corridor outside his room — in two lines, side by side. This is what many teachers do, and in itself it is not poor practice. But with the geography teacher, negative interchanges between him and the children began with this. Waiting quietly was not enough; the children could not enter the room until there was total silence. This sometimes took four or five minutes, and what the teacher did not seem to realise was that it gave some intrepid spirits an excellent opportunity to trick him into a kind of game. They would shelter behind a taller child and make just enough noise to prevent their entrance into the classroom, but not enough to be identified and punished. Indeed, many of the interchanges between the geography teacher and his classes took the form of ritualised games. Invariably this period of waiting was a negative introduction to the lesson.

It was sometimes compounded by his poor time keeping. The class inside the room did not emerge when the bell rang, because their lesson was not ended. When they did come out, and when another class was waiting to go in, the temptation to take advantage of the crowded corridor was too much for the less well-behaved children. Thus, even before the lesson began, there were opportunities for unruly behaviour.

When the lesson did begin, some children who had been criticised for their behaviour outside the room were already in trouble. If the lesson was late in starting, the teacher expressed his irritation, but the lateness was not really due to the children. It came about because of his own behaviour. It was not long before further interruptions prevented some of the class from starting work, and another ritual began. As the children had to draw maps, and as the teacher was insistent about neatness, the matter of clean hands soon arose. Any child whose hands were not clean enough was sent outside to wash them. This the children knew well and they played the game according to the rules. Once in the toilets, the rule was to stay as long as possible and have as much fun as the environment could provide. The child who had been noisy outside the door, and whose hands were not clean enough to participate in the lesson without a visit to the toilets was publicly criticised twice in the first ten minutes of the lesson. The teacher's comments were frequently sarcastic with references to 'not knowing about soap and water' and to 'queuing outside bingo halls'. Such a child also discovered that he or she need do no geography whatsoever for as long as 15 minutes! Of course, children should wait quietly outside classroom doors and should have clean hands, but the teacher went about achieving this in ways that made it less probable that children would be quiet and clean.

There were other opportunities for the children to delay and interrupt the flow of the lesson. When atlases and paper had to be distributed, the teacher would ask the monitors to give them out. The fact that he did not know who these were would not have mattered, but with a strange perversity he would say: 'Monitors, give out the atlases — who are the monitors in this class?' When this led to the sort of wrangles that frequently arise with poorly organised classes, he would make further criticisms of the children, exclaiming: 'You lot cannot even remember who the monitors are', and overlooking the fact that he could not either. These interchanges were not lost on the children, who made the best use they could of the delays to the lesson. When the work of copying maps or diagrams was under way, he would walk around the class as the maths and craft teachers did, but his comments on the work he saw were frequently negative and challenging. They varied more, according to his perceptions of the children than to the work they had done. For those whose behaviour he found acceptable, he would express any criticism mildly. For those whom he considered 'thick', the criticisms were expressed in more extreme terms. 'What do you call that, then?' 'A 5-year-old would do better.' 'Take that out and throw it in the basket with the other rubbish.'

A noticeable feature of the behaviour of the geography teacher was his attachment to the long pointer, which he carried around the room with him. He did not ever use this to strike the children, and he needed it to point to details on the large maps in his room, but he did not put it aside when he no longer needed it. He would use it to point at children, and sometimes, as an extension of his arm, he would turn the pages of their books with it as he walked around the classroom. In their criticisms of him, they referred to his use of this pointer, his sarcasm and his pedantic adherence to very high standards of behaviour as features they disliked most about him. It was not enough for them to be quiet – he insisted on silence. It was not enough to raise a hand in answer to a question – the arm had to be kept still and perpendicular. The cumulative effect of all this attention to detail was that a great deal of time was wasted in his lessons. The frequent hold-ups while he 'sorted someone out' for a relative minor infringement of his rules added to the irritation that could almost be felt in the geography room. These hold-ups also had the effect of so slowing down the lessons that they ran over the time allotted.

Inevitably, he provoked children into confrontations. His physique and his demeanour prevented these from escalating to the point where he was ever threatened with any physical violence, but there were unpleasant incidents in the classroom which he overcame by peremptorily despatching a child from his room. He would not push a confrontation too far and showed considerable skill at disengaging at the point of crisis – usually going to the classroom door, opening it and pointing to the corridor. This was the signal for the child concerned to leave the room, and he or she usually did. It seemed that the lessons were such that no child much minded whether they stayed in them or left them. This attitude of indifference was expressed by third and fourth-year children – they did not think he was worth their while. The younger children did not bear much ill will if they were ordered out of the room. They had gone through the processes of confronting him and accepted the outcome.

The geography teacher illustrated many of the characteristics that Hargreaves has identified as common to 'deviance-provocative' teachers (Hargreaves *et al.*, 1975). These are:

> assuming that children whom they define as deviant do not wish to work, and will avoid it whenever possible;
> believing that it is not reasonable for them to provide conditions under which they will work, if these are different from the conditions under which other children work successfully;
> believing that discipline is a contest between teachers and children that the teacher must win;
> inability to defuse tense situations;
> frequently issuing ultimatums;
> believing in the value of confrontations and becoming involved in them;

considering children as being anti-authority and anti-school rules;
neglecting deviant children in interactions in the classroom;
punishing inconsistently;
expecting children, especially deviant children (or those whom they
perceived as deviant) to behave badly;
making many negative evaluations on deviant children – to them
and to colleagues;
being sarcastic;
believing that children, on the whole, are not to be trusted, and
deviant children certainly are not;
avoiding informal contacts with children outside the classroom.

The belief that discipline is a kind of contest between them and the
children that they must win is not an uncommon belief among teachers.
It is not so much incorrect as imprecise. It is imprecise because it arises
through an incorrect understanding of what discipline is. It is
frequently confused with management, order, obedience, the results of
training and with conformity. But it is more than these; it is inseparable
from relationships between teachers and children, and, in classrooms
particularly, it is inseparable from classroom processes – the ways in
which learning tasks are prepared, presented and structured. But it is
frequently spoken of as if it were a commodity – one that some teachers have and some, alas, have not. When teachers say about a
colleague: 'He has no discipline' or 'She should exert more discipline',
this idea of discipline as a commodity is given emphasis. This misperception of what discipline is was well illustrated by a teacher who said that
he was in charge of discipline in the third and fourth years of a school.
But no one can be in charge of discipline in that way, as if it were foot-
balls. Saying that someone is in charge of discipline is as confusing as
saying the vicar is in charge of honesty in the parish. The vicar can
influence the honesty of those with whom he is in contact – who may
or may not be tempted into dishonest behaviour – most effectively,
if he is present when the temptation to behave dishonestly arises, or if
his relationships with the tempted remind them of his attitudes.

Two features of the geography teacher's classroom management are
worth further comment. He was correct in his ideas of quietness, of
clean hands, of orderly behaviour. But his efforts to secure these desirable outcomes were prevented by his negative attitudes to children.
Much of what he wanted them to do they would have done quickly
enough, if he had not been sarcastic and ready to denigrate them. In
his complaint that the children did not behave or learn as he wanted
them to, he could not see that he actively prevented the behaviour and

learning he wanted. He managed, after a fashion, the confrontations he stirred up, but he did not take into account the uselessness of them. They recurred with the same children with all the wasted time and frustration involved.

In reviewing the classroom management of the three teachers described, it is tempting to the inexperienced to attribute the successes of the maths teacher or the craft teacher to their personalities or their charismatic qualities. It is true that some teachers are more fortunate than others, in that they have more humour, or more enthusiasm and more infectious pleasantness. But when charismatic teachers are closely observed, it is possible to discern that they enjoy what they are doing. This is not only enjoyment of their subject — they enjoy being with children and understand what they can do together. This is not because they are childish, but because they respect children as children. They deploy skills which the percipient observer can identify. The maths teacher did certain things and avoided doing others that made his classroom management effective — as did the craft teacher. The geography teacher did things and neglected others which the other two teachers would have avoided and practised respectively. Both maths and craft teachers set up a classroom environment which cued the children into the behaviour and performance they wanted. This is the foundation of a 'good atmosphere' in a classroom — the presence of various cues to the desired behaviour and performance. When a good atmosphere is there, it is more difficult for a disruptive child to break it, and one of the reasons for this is that the teacher does not break it. With the geography teacher, these positive cues could hardly be said to exist. In fact, the cues in his lessons were more the other way round — the children constantly picked up cues which suggested to them how they could provoke or disrupt. They took their cues from him, who provoked them by his comments and disrupted their work by his behaviour.

8 CONFRONTATION IN THE CLASSROOM: CHILDREN WITH PROBLEMS

On the whole, it is wise for teachers to avoid confrontations with children when these can be avoided, but there are those occasions when a confrontation cannot be avoided and those occasions when it can be beneficial. A teacher cannot avoid a confrontation if she is summoned by a colleague to help in some crisis which was nothing to do with her. The angry child may turn on the summoned teacher and continue with her what he began with her colleague. There are some circumstances when a teacher may decide that he is not going to put up with some child's provocative or stupid behaviour any longer, or that he is going to demonstrate to a child who continually bullies or teases other children that he has met his match. A confrontation with such a child would be beneficial to the child concerned, to the other children who witnessed it, and to the teacher's management. But there are certain considerations that should guide the teacher in making this decision. If he is convinced that the confrontation would be beneficial, he has next to be sure that he can manage it, if, once it has started, the child continues in his defiance or provocation, and — if the worst comes to the worst — that he can manage the child, should he attempt to present the teacher with a physical challenge. Once started, confrontations sometimes develop very quickly, as described in Chapter 9, and it would be foolish to bring on a confrontation with a child and then have to seek help from a stronger colleague. When confrontations are considered to be necessary, they should be deliberate and properly managed so that they do not deteriorate into undignified examples of child hostility and teacher counter-hostility.

Some teachers, either through their anxiety or inexperience, blunder into confrontations which they cannot manage and which are of no value to the child concerned, to them, or to the class. Others seek them without proper occasion. These confrontations have nothing to commend them.

Avoiding Confrontations

When thinking about ways in which teachers might avoid unhelpful confrontations, it may be helpful to think about classes with reference to their stability or instability. When observing effective teachers with a class, one of the noticeable features of well-conducted lessons is the way in which the teachers do not allow the stability of the class to be threatened or upset by one or two children in it. Neither do they upset this stability themselves – as very anxious teachers tend to and as provocative teachers do. The maths teacher and the craft teacher, described in Chapter 7, in their different ways did not allow destabilising factors to upset their classes, whereas the geography teacher constantly introduced destabilising factors himself, both by his own behaviour and in his interactions with children.

In any school, there are likely to be events, over which teachers have no control and which they cannot prevent, that upset the stability of classes. There are staff absences, which mean that a teacher is called upon to cover for an absent colleague. They do not know the children whom they are suddenly called upon to teach, and they may not be familiar with the lesson material the children expect. An unfortunate aspect of this situation is that the very children who are likely to be difficult to manage are those who tend to be poor at adapting to unexpected changes in routine, or variations in deployment of staff. There are times when building contractors and decorators are present in schools, interrupting classes with the noise they make and disturbing timetable arrangements. It is in circumstances like these that the stability of groups are threatened and confrontations are more likely to arise, unless teachers are particularly wary in their interactions with children who cannot cope with distraction nor adapt to unexpected change. Nor is it only the children whose functioning is impaired by such events. They may cause exasperation and frutration in teachers, so that they are less able to bear with any signs of unacceptable behaviour. Such negative situations are very frequently sources of confrontations.

As we have seen in Chapter 6, the ways in which very anxious teachers behave are also likely to upset the stability of a class. They do not mean to upset the stability of a class and they have little chance of managing successfully when they do. Their behaviour may bring on confrontation by accident: they unwittingly provoke a child or fall into a trap which a child prepares for them. In Chapter 9, this blundering into a confrontation is looked at in more detail.

It is not only outside events, or very anxious teachers, or those who deliberately provoke children that threaten the stability of a class (and frequently do destabilise it) so that confrontations are more likely to arise. Certain children have strong tendencies to do this; they either do it themselves or are the cause of it in others. Among these, the most noticeable are children with marked difficulties of adjustment; those who are seriously underachieving, who are frustrated by their failures and very sensitive about them; the unpopular child, who may also be a 'victim child'; the child whose behaviour may not be acceptable to teachers, but who is the licensed wag or buffoon; and the saboteur. The probabilities of confrontation are increased, if teachers are not aware of the presence of such children in a class, nor aware of ways of managing them.

The Child with Difficulties of Adjustment

Behavioural psychologists have helped teachers to realise that many incidents of disruptive or inappropriate behaviour are specific to partic-ular situations, to particular individuals and to particlar environments (Ullman and Krasner, 1965; Leach and Raybould, 1977; Hallahan and Kauffman, 1978; Roe, 1978). They emphasise that features in the environment act as stimuli, making disruptive behaviour more probable, and that contingent reinforcing events will either establish this behaviour or reduce it and extinguish it. This explanation has helped teachers to recognise that much inappropriate behaviour is not endo-genous, and that they can arrange classroom environments that will significantly reduce the behaviours preventing children's learning and social progress. Application of the principles of applied behaviour analysis and the use of behaviour-modification techniques such as those described in Chapter 4 have undoubtedly helped teachers to find ways of establishing effective methods of classroom control.

Excellent as these techniques are, however, it is important for teachers to recognise that many children whose disruptive behaviour is a persistent problem have had experiences of other people and of themselves which go a long way to account for the difficulties they cause. This is not to deny that the actual classroom environment may or may not increase their tendency to misbehave, but rather to emphasise that there are factors outside the control of teachers which make these children more likely than others to become the cause of instability in the classroom. Their need for counselling and support, for assessment of their problems at home, help for their parents and the involvement of supportive personnel from outside the school show that their prob-lems are not of management alone.

Among disruptive children are those whose experiences of parent figures have led them to regard themselves as unworthy and undeserving. Because they were neither wanted nor loved they have not been esteemed by those whom they might legitimately expect to esteem them. Consequently they do not esteem themselves. We know that a negative self-concept seriously interferes with children's functioning. The experiences of alienation and of failure — not only in school-based learning tasks, but in their relationships and in many social situations — are just the negative experiences many disruptive children have had. Among the older ones especially, it is little use for teachers who find themselves in conflict with them to appeal to their self-respect, for they have very little, and what they do have needs careful nurturing before any meaningful reference can be made to it. At the same time, they are not much influenced by punishment, because overfamiliarity with it has made them indifferent. Although some children who have had long experience of neglect and deprivation seek punishment, because it is at least one way of gaining attention, the punishment does nothing to alter their behaviour for the better. Indeed, it is more likely to increase the probability of unwanted behaviour, because it brings about some reward to the child, unpleasant though that may appear to be.

The experiences of such children have affected them in other ways, which show in their behaviour in school. Not only do they perceive themselves as unworthy and undeserving, they also tend to perceive adults in authority as potentially uncaring and hostile. This perception has developed because of their experiences of the behaviour of hostile and uncaring adults in their own environments, it has led them to displace the hostility they feel towards these adults on to teachers, who have to frustrate them, as they do when they control them.Whereas most children, however much they protest, usually accept criticism or punishment as fair, and they are able to make the necessary connections between the punishment and their responsibility for it, this is not the case for those disruptive children who do not perceive themselves and others as more fortunate children do. Because they have not been able to trust others, and because their relationshps with others have been impaired by the destructive influences of rejection and hostility, they are much more likely to regard punishment as evidence of vindictiveness or spite. Redl (1971), in his comments on punishment, and Redl and Wineman (1951 and 1952) have given illuminating accounts of the attitudes that over-punished and under-esteemed children have towards teachers to whom they present difficult problems of management.

Mention already has been made of discipline as an inter-personal matter. Teachers agree that they have little chance of managing classes successfully unless they establish positive relationships with some of the children in them, and hopefully with all of them. The children who are so often in the worst kind of trouble in schools are those with whom the staff complain that they are unable to make any meaningful contact. It is a feature of children with problems of adjustment that they find the making and the sustaining of good relationships with others difficult, and some of them never succeed in doing this. They are either too demanding and too impetuous, or too passive and dependent. They give way to temper and to anger, which other children find distasteful or frightening. They are selfish and inconsiderate, or ingratiating and clinging. They are wary of making relationships with adults, as their relationship with some of them have caused them a great deal of pain or unhappiness in the past, when they were let down or rejected by others on whom they relied for affection and support. When they have some evidence to believe that some adult — perhaps a teacher who shows concern for them and who teaches them in a subject where their motiviation is high — cares about them, many of these children behave in ways that seem paradoxical and self-destructive. They exhibit towards this adult their most unattractive and demanding character-istics. This does not always happen when such children perceive in a friendly teacher the understanding patience or concern which they most seek and need. They react positively to this teacher and show unusual co-operation. But when the opposite happens, due to the degree and persistence of their deprivation, and they put the relation-ship to severe tests, this is perplexing and wounding to the teacher concerned. At the conscious level, it seems that such children are declar-ing that they have heard expressions of goodwill many times before, but, as this goodwill was withdrawn rapidly when they made demands upon it, they will see how the teacher can stand up to such demands. They then proceed to make these demands, some of which are aimed at those particular vulnerabilities in the teacher that their suspicious and active interest has discovered. It is when this happens that teachers are heard to remark that as they tried kindness and the child took advantage of it, this is evidence that their approach will not succeed. When this happens, it is not only sad for the teacher concerned, but it is sad for the child, because it strengthens the belief that they are unlikeable and others are hostile. It strengthens their reliance upon what Redl and Wineman have described as the deprived child's delusional system, in which their per-ception of themselves and of other people is distorted by their previous experiences. They have succeeded in dragging into their contemporary relationships just those features which destroyed previous ones, and they have manipulated benevolent people into behaving towards them as they did not mean to behave. If this process continues, their reactions towards others harden into fixed patterns of behaviour which are not quickly or easily changed.

Sometimes such hostile behaviour is motivated by feelings of revenge, as Rudolph Dreikurs has pointed out (Dreikurs, 1968). Deprived, alienated children are likely to feel revengeful because of the treatment they have received in the past from those who failed them in their relationships and acted with hostility towards them. Here the process of displacement shows itself. The hostility they feel towards significant figures in their own environment alights on those who stand in for the rejecting or uncaring person, usually a parent who is too formidable for them to risk declaring their true feeling of hostility. Many children with problems of adjustment have a limited repertoire of behavioural responses anyway, and in this repertoire, displacement and projection — the abscribing to others their own shortcomings and weaknesses — are too ready at hand. Their fixity of response limits their adaptability. They behave in inappropriate and unsatisfying ways, in circumstances that better-adjusted children perceive as requiring the adaptive responses they are capable of, and they seem particularly inept at differentiating between people and circumstances.

There is another explanation of such inappropriate, hostile and unacceptable behaviour. Some children have learned to behave in the ways that they do. In the face of disappointment, frustration or denial, they copy or imitate the ways in which their parents or other significant figures behave. Not only do they witness this behaviour in models in their environment, they are aware that such behaviour brings its rewards. The father who vents his frustrations at home relies on this to bring about the attention or solace he needs. Siblings who make demands because of their jealousy or envy of other family members are given attention to pacify them. They themselves are indulged or gratified, according to the frequency and intensity of their demanding behaviour. In the true sense of the term, these children have never learned to behave properly.

Fortunately, there are not many such children in the ordinary school system, but there are some and teachers meet with them. In many ways, they resemble many maladjusted children and the advice given to teachers of these children by Laslett (1977 and 1982), Herbert (1978), Saunders (1979) and Wilson and Evans (1980), is helpful to teachers who have to manage these children in their classes. Although it is not true that all maladjusted children present their teachers with problems of management, many do. They are disruptive and unstable members of classes. For many of them, the excitement and inevitable attention that goes with challenging a teacher is an irresistible temptation. They delight in drawing teachers into confrontations and they are skilled at bringing about their defeat in them.

The Underachieving Child

Other children who may threaten the stability of a class group are those who are seriously behind in their acquisition of basic educational skills, and who are sensitive about their failures. Although it is convenient to discuss these children separately from the children who show marked problems of adjustment, educational difficulties are common to both. In their surveys of 9- to 11-year-olds in the Isle of Wight, Rutter and his fellow authors found that a large proportion of the children with behaviour disorders were 28 months retarded in their reading (Rutter, Tizard and Whitmore, 1970), and evidence from the Schools Council project on the education of disturbed children supports these findings (Wilson and Evans, 1980). In many children, their difficulties in reading lead them into compensatory behaviour, which, as it is so frequently attention seeking, is not acceptable. In others, their anxieties and frustrations prevent them from acquiring skills in reading. These connections between reading failure and behaviour disorder are reasonably straightforward, but the authors of the Isle of Wight studies also suggest that there may be a factor in some children's personality that is responsible for both their academic and social difficulties.

Of all failures in acquiring basic educational skills, children are most sensitive about their failures in reading. It is this which is such a blow to their self-esteem, even among those who make out that they do not care whether they can read or not. This is borne out in the remarks that adults make about their schooldays. Of the many who may declare publicly that they never understood maths and most of the maths instruction went over their heads, there are very few who admit to not being able to read. This is certainly true of children, and many of them go to great lengths to hide their reading difficulties, unless they are confident that they can rely on the sympathy of those to whom they disclose them.

It is because reading failure is such an embarrassment to a child that an unwary teacher might stumble into a confrontation with him, because of her ignorance of the child's predicament, if she asks him to read aloud. The last thing the child wants is to have his failure made public. If it is, it is unlikely that the child, especially one in the secondary school, will quietly say to the teacher:' Please miss, I can't read.' What is more probable is that he will either make a stumbling start on the passage that he is asked to read and hope to be rescued by the teacher's awareness of his predicament, or reply to the request that he reads aloud with some comment that the teacher considers to be impertinent. If he does make a start and the teacher realises his predicament, then there is a simple way for them both out of the situation. But if his fluster and anxiety leads him to respond with a provocative comment, as fluster and anxiety frequently do, and if the unsuspecting teacher reacts to that with indignation or criticism, then a path leading into a confrontation quickly opens up. This exchange may be the first step up the 'escalation-detonation staircase' that is described in Chapter 9.

It is in his response to the teacher's request to read that the non-reader may be seen to threaten the stability of the class. This would be aggravated if he is, at the same time, a child who has difficulties in his relationship with other children. Another child may make some slighting comment on the non-reader, who flares up at the comment, so that the teacher is suddenly faced with a quarrel. The compensatory behaviour of the non-reader who, if he cannot shine in acceptable ways, is determined to seek recognition, even if this brings about some unpleasant consequences, is another threat to class stability. However this threat arises, the best way to prevent it is for the teacher to be aware, as soon as possible, of which children in a class are sensitive to their failure in reading or in other basic subjects of the curriculum. In her own class, this presents no problems. Difficulties arise when she has to cover for an absent colleague or never does have an opportunity to find out as much as she would like about a class that she teaches.

The Victim Child

The victim child is also likely to threaten the stability of a class of children. He is unlikely to draw a teacher into a confrontation, but may well be the source of one involving another child. He is the boy who is continually teased, or bullied, or taken advantage of by other children, and who, according to his perception of these events, is the innocent victim. It is true that bullies will attack those who are weaker than they are, however the victim of the attack behaves, but with the victim child, there are aspects of his behaviour which elicit aggressive behaviour in others. He is usually unaware that this is so. He knows that he is unpopular, but he cannot account for his unpopularity. Hostile reactions to his behaviour may arise from his irritating ways — he is forever interfering or giving unwanted advice. He may make undue demands upon the friendship of other children, wanting to have another member of the class as a friend to the exclusion of other children, showing jealousy of any other friend his companion has. He may be a chatterbox and a sneak. He may be fussy, over-dependent and so poor in his personal organisation that friendship with him is a burden. Whatever it is about him, he makes undue demands on the tolerance and goodwill of other children, so that his companionship is insufficiently rewarding for them to overlook his shortcomings. Other children will not tolerate from him what they meet with equanimity in others. It is this intolerance of others of him, rather than what he does himself, that makes him a threat to group stability. He is likely to do or say something that is too much for the self-control of another child and to become the centre of angry exchanges in the classroom.

A teacher may best help such a child, and therefore his control over the class, by pointing out to him that he cannot continue forever to blame other children for his misfortunes and that he should begin to look at his own behaviour. It is probable that at the start of such a discussion, the boy will stoutly deny that the fault is in him, and it is not unlikely that long periods of denial will have convinced him that this is so. In denying his own responsibility for his unpopularity and his misfortunes, he is not telling untruths; he is bolstering himself against what he suspects is the truth, which is not easy to face. Sometimes victim children can be helped if a teacher calls upon whatever friend he has to add an opinion to the teacher's, and children will frequently listen to their peers with more belief than to teachers. Such a child can be helped by teacher intervention, when he observes the child saying things or doing things that will inevitably bring trouble on his head — the teacher's part in this would not be to prevent the other children's hostile reaction to him, but rather to draw the boy's attention to the fact that he is provoking them again.

A behaviour-modification programme would fit in very appropriately for this kind of behaviour, as a teacher can easily devise one in which the boy is regularly rewarded for his successes in not being made a victim. If the teacher adopts another approach and is concerned about the possibility of the masochistic qualities of his behaviour, then he might refer the boy to somebody who could counsel him at the level appropriate for him to explore this behaviour and bring it under control.

The situation of the child with physical, mental or sensory handicap is not quite the same as the victim child who elicits hostility or rejection in other children. There is the possibility that such children will be teased or shunned by other children, but studies of integration programmes show that this does not happen very frequently (Chazan *et al*., 1981; Hegarty, Pocklington and Lucas, 1982).

The Trapped-in-Role Child

In many classes, there is one child who is the class buffoon or wit, or one who dares to try the teacher's patience beyond reasonable bounds. She is not a teacher-baiter in the usual meaning of this term and is not usually set upon a confrontation, although one may develop from her behaviour. What is at work here is more subtle and less sinister. It has more to do with her relationships with the group and theirs with her, than her relationship with the teacher. She is uncertain of her status in the group and believes she can enhance this by drawing children's attention to her boldness. She is uncertain of her status with teachers, unless she brings herself to their attention. She is, in fact, uncertain of herself. She discovers that her ready wit or her intrepid behaviour wins group approval and ensures popularity with her peers. Her behaviour is less welcome to teaching staff and has a certain price which is sometimes exacted, but, on the whole, the status she acquires is worth the cost. It brings attention, it gives some recognition which she may not be able to achieve in more acceptable ways, and it is exciting. Sooner or later she is the licensed wit, and the description is an interesting one. The other children give her this licence, because her behaviour is not without some value to them. If she oversteps the mark, they lose patience with her, and they withdraw the licence, but she manages well enough within the rules as they are understood in the class. By various messages, sometimes overt and sometimes covert, the group of children sustain her in her role.

After a time, the girl woud like to give up her role. It is inconvenient and, as she develops better ways of functioning and gaining attention, it is no longer necessary. But she cannot do this alone — her wish to change is not enough. The group has to change in their relationships with her and allow her to leave the role she no longer wants nor needs. Her attempts to change are not sufficient to overcome group expectations. They do not easily surrender the satisfaction that her behaviour gives them. Now the girl is in a dilemma. She has to rework her relationships with the group and put them on a sounder basis, and repair her relationships with staff. She needs help to do this. The help that she needs will be more easily given, if teachers are aware of the group dynamics that produce this situation, for it is an aspect of the behaviour of groups, as Irene Caspari (1976) has made clear. It is not uncommon for a teacher to become involved in a confrontation with such a girl whose humourous sallies or impertinence goads them into an angry response. As with the non-reader who reacts negatively to what seems to be a reasonable request, the angry response may be the first step up the escalation-detonation staircase. Such a confrontation can be avoided if the teacher, aware of what the girl is doing in response to group pressure, and what the class is doing for their own satisfaction, shows that he is aware of these processes and discusses them with all the parties involved. This will be much more effective than continual expressions of irritation or anger with the girl.

The Saboteur

There is another child who threatens to upset the balance of a class and for whom a teacher is well advised to be prepared. He is the saboteur, a child who enjoys the drama of a teacher in conflict with another child or other children, even if he does not escape from such conflicts unscathed. He is not as noticeable as the boy or girl with more obvious signs of adjustment difficulties and does not give way to openly disruptive behaviour, but he has developed strategies for irritating other children and egging them on towards confrontation. He will defeat a teacher's intention to ignore the provocative behaviour of other children by drawing attention to it. He knows just what to say or do when he observes a classroom crisis on the wane so that it may start up again. If a child subsides from a temper outburst, he manages to provoke him into another. If a quarrel subsides, he knows what comments will rekindle it. If he observes a teacher struggling with her irritation, because of the behaviour of some child in the class, he will succeed in ensuring that she fails in the attempt. A good deal of his subversive and devious behaviour goes on in playgrounds or corridors, when no teacher is at hand to intervene. He is dextrous in avoiding the consequences of his own behaviour and successful in drawing teachers into confrontations. In some ways, he is like a ferret who works under-

ground, as he whispers to one child about another or makes provocative comments about a teacher from behind the raised lid of his desk.

In managing a saboteur, it is better if a teacher avoids questioning
him about what he does or has done, because he enjoys the opportunity
this presents to make whatever capital he can from the occasion. If the
teacher makes any error in his accusations, then he seizes the opportunity to deny that he did what the teacher knows he did, but did not
recount it accurately. One exasperated teacher related the dialogue
which followed the late arrival in his class of a child he had seen a few
minutes earlier combing her hair before a mirror in the domestic science
room. When she did arrive, and the teacher asked why she had stopped
'to comb her hair in the mirror', the girl replied that she had not been
combing her hair in the mirror. This flat denial and untruth which the
girl repeated during the exchange made the teacher increasingly angry.
The naughty girl at last announced that she had not been combing her
hair *in* the mirror because that was impossible! It is this kind of cool and
exasperating exchange that demonstrates the dangers of involving such
children in questioning, and it is best avoided. The mounting irritation
in the dispute is just what the saboteurs enjoy. It is better to tell them
what they have done, and to make sure that there are no possibilities for
ingenious word play. It is also reassuring to other children, many of
whom have reasons to regret the saboteur's activities, to perceive that the
teacher is ahead of the game and has kept the initiative. Such antici-
patory observations prevents the saboteur from drawing a teacher into a
confrontation which, at its close, was probably not worth the time
spent on it. If the behaviour is worth a confrontation, then a teacher
would be well advised to make it when he is not flustered by the
approach to it which the child has prepared.

A knowledge of the behaviour patterns of children who threaten the
stability of a class prevents those confrontations which impair, rather
than improve, a teacher's management. In their own classes, teachers
have time to know the children well enough to avoid useless and ill-
considered confrontations. When this time is limited, for whatever
reasons, it is advisable for teachers to pause and to reflect on the
possible motives for a disruptive child's behaviour, so that the poorly
adjusted child, the frustrated and sensitive non-reader, or the licensed
wag, the victim child and the saboteur do not trap them into a situation which moves, often very swiftly, into the opening stages of an ill-
advised confrontation.

9 CONFRONTATION IN THE CLASSROOM: TEACHER STRATEGIES

When we consider the variety of factors that affect the interactions between teachers and classes, it becomes plain that it is not possible to suggest ways in which teachers can always manage to avoid unnecessary and unhelpful confrontations. The most that anyone at a distance from the classroom can do is to suggest guidelines which might help teachers to avoid those confrontations that serve no useful purpose and, at worst, result in consequences which they did not foresee and which they regret. In some circumstances, usually when there is tension in a classroom, it only needs a teacher to say the wrong thing, or do the wrong thing, for him to find that he has a confrontation on his hands for which he is not prepared and which he did not want. The guidelines, if followed, should reduce this possibility.

Guidelines for Avoiding Confrontations

Avoiding Public Denigration of a Child

Although criticism of some children cannot be avoided, it is a mistake for a teacher loudly and publicly to denigrate a child. This stirs up resentment and hostility and, even if the child dare not express this openly, it sours her relationships with the teacher. It is a poor example of adult behaviour. If the child is addressed in unmeasured tones, she loses face with her peers and she then has the problem of putting this right. If she redresses the balance by some verbal attack on the teacher, then this may be the starting point of a confrontation. Children, especially older children, resent being 'bawled out' as much as adults do and, like adults, they particularly resent any sarcasm that accompanies such comments. For a teacher to use her superior wit and readiness with words is really a form of bullying, and it is as unpleasant and as likely to stir up hostility as physical bullying does.

Children are surprisingly unanimous in their comments about teachers' behaviour. They do not mind strict teachers, so long as they are not nasty as well (Mills, 1976; Meighan, 1978), and they do not mind being made to work and to behave. It is the overbearing and sarcastic teacher who is unpopular. Some teachers, of course, are given to sarcasm, but many sarcastic teachers speak in the way that they do because of their anxiety and lack of self-confidence. For these teachers, letting slip a sarcastic comment is particularly unfortunate, if it sets off a crisis they do not want and cannot manage.

Ignoring Behaviour

The advantages of 'planned ignoring' have already been mentioned in Chapter 2. It is worth while to emphasise that planned ignoring is not the same as overlooking behaviour because the teacher cannot do anything else.

Only the teacher in the classroom knows whether he can ignore behaviour or not. It would not have been appropriate for the history teacher to ignore Martin's comment that began the confrontation described later in this chapter, although he could have responded to it more wisely than he did. Ignoring provocative behaviour need not be complete ignoring – a teacher may ignore a provocative comment when it is made, and return to it when the child is deflated by the teacher's lack of response. Nor need the ignoring be complete. One of the disconcerting reactions of the maths teacher described in Chapter 7 – disconcerting to the child, that is – was his way of looking at someone who said the wrong thing or did the wrong thing, and making no comment. While he looked, he may have been thinking about Euclid, or he may have been deciding whether or not to have recourse to his well-known notebook. The child could not be certain. Although this ignoring is not quite what behavioural psychologists usually mean by ignoring unwanted behaviour, it was very effective. However, it went with his whole battery of management strategies. It is unlikely that a teacher will *establish* his authority by ignoring all the behaviour he finds unacceptable. He must have, and have demonstrated, other strategies for managing unwanted behaviour.

Awareness of the Effects on Non-Verbal Communication

It is very easy for a teacher, especially if she is angry, to forget the effects of non-verbal communications. For some children, these communicate a challenge which they take up. For others, they show that the teacher is flustered and they take advantage of this. Many confrontations begin, or are maintained, not only by what a teacher says, but by the way she walks or strides towards a child, glares at him or points at him. Once a confrontation starts, it is the angry presence of the teacher close to a child that acts as a powerful irritant in the situation and prolongs or sharpens the crisis. In the confrontation described later in this chapter, the history teacher would have saved much of the trouble, if he had stepped back from the boy who saw his presence as a challenge, as indeed it was. The geography teacher described in Chapter 7, with all his faults, had sufficient control of himself to step away from the child he provoked.

Avoiding Physical Intervention

A very common feature of some crises in the classroom, which makes a confrontation much more probable, is a teacher's attempting to grab hold of some object a child has that is causing a disturbance. In these circumstances, especially if the teacher is bigger and stronger than the child, it is tempting for him to make a grab at the transistor radio, or whatever it is that the child has and that he has refused to surrender when asked. The teacher may be successful, but grabbing at the radio, or pushing the child to get hold of it, moves the crisis into a much more unpredictable dimension. It may very quickly become the first step in the confrontation with little chance of escaping from it.

The child with the radio may begin the tantalising game of moving it out of the teacher's reach. There is no end to this catch-as-catch-can manoeuvre. Each move in it increases the teacher's discomfort, increases the child's satisfaction and adds to the tension. For the spectators in the class, it is hard to beat as a diverting spectacle. For the teacher, it is hard to beat as an exasperating and undignified display of impotence. He may succeed in loosening the child's grip on the radio, but it then falls and is damaged. The situation has now taken a turn for the worse. Although the child was in the wrong, the damaged radio has complicated the situation and lessened the distinction between the rights and wrongs of it. The teacher will be accused of damaging the radio, and although this is not fair and it is certainly not what he intended, he has given a hostage to fortune. If the radio was a treasured possession, the boy who owned it may be so incensed by the damage to it that he will turn on the teacher and his language or his behaviour then makes a confrontation probable. In the ensuing mêlée, with its unpredictable consequences, the original offence is lost sight of. At the end of it all, the trigger that began the swift march of events was the teacher's impatient grab at the radio. This did not cause the crisis — the child did that by having the radio and not giving it up when asked to. But the grabbing and pushing moved the crisis towards the confrontation.

The Open University film *It All Depends upon Your Point of View* demonstrates the dangers of a teacher making a physical intervention. A teacher goes to take a fountain pen from a girl, who raises her hand with the pen in it. This action releases ink from the pen so that it sprays out across the girl's blouse. Shouting 'It's all your fault!' she either hits the teacher or the teacher hits her, or the teacher's face hits her hand, or it doesn't, or whatever. In the moment of confrontation, brought on by the teacher grabbing at the pen, no one knows what happened — who struck whom, who struck first, whose hand got in the way, whose face was in the way. This confusion and panic, which so often go with attempted physical interventions, emphasise that they are best avoided.

Apologising

It is not uncommon to see a teacher make a blunder in classroom management — perhaps by accusing a child unjustly, or snapping at a child who is not the real culprit — to be patently in the wrong, and then to compound the error by persisting, when an apology would have avoided a confrontation.

It is not demeaning to make an apology. Teachers are not super people. They are human beings and human beings make mistakes, especially when they are under stress. If a teacher is really in the wrong, then it is courteous, as it shows respect for children, if she apologises to them. It is what teachers teach children to do and what they expect them to do. If they do not apologise when they are in the wrong, it is not because they are like that as people, but because they have the strange notion that they weaken their authority if they admit to fallibility.

It is better to be open about an apology. To hum and haw, and then say: 'Well, perhaps I owe you an apology' is easier than saying: 'I am sorry; I was mistaken,' but it is less fair and it is less likely to disarm an offended and potentially disruptive child.

Escalation and Detontation in Confrontations

We have already seen that there are usually some children in classes whose behaviour makes a confrontation more probable. When teachers know who such children are, they can adapt their approaches to them to avoid conflict, or use whatever methods they find appropriate to temper the wind to the shorn lamb. It sometimes happens, however, that a teacher will stir up a confrontation because she does not know of the antecedent events that affect a child's reactions to reproof or criticism. When this does happen, and when the matter is discussed afterwards, then one hears such phrases as: 'If only I had known she was worried about her sister' or 'I wish I had known he had just had a flare up with . . . '

The confrontation described below is an ugly and serious one, but it is not one unknown in many classrooms. The teacher concerned made a reasonable request to a boy, but he has, unknowingly, stumbled against a boy whose mood at the time, arising from events over which the teacher had no control, made it important for the teacher to avoid any provocative comments or hasty actions. The teacher's manner unfortunately aggravated the situation that arose in the classroom, and this swiftly moved into a confrontation that went out of control. The serious consequences were not altogether due to mood or antecedent events. The teacher made mistakes, and the boy contributed his measure of unpleasant behaviours. One of the sad features of the confrontation was that both the teacher and the boy regretted what they had done, but it was too late. In his comments on conflicts between teachers and children, Pik (1981) has drawn attention to the sadness that teachers feel when the consequences of some upset in a classroom are more serious than they intended them to be, and these feelings are very real. In some ways, ugly confrontations with serious consequences are like accidents. They happen very quickly, and the situations of those concerned after they have happened are dramatically different from their situations before they began. They also illustrate the maxim that great things arise from little ones, but not because of them.

The boy concerned was reasonable enough in school. He was a third-year boy, and there was no evidence that he had problems of adjustment. He had the usual uncertainties of mood associated with adolescence, but on the whole he was pleasant and co-operative. However, on the morning of the confrontation, matters had not gone well for him, and the history lesson was at a climax of unfortunate events. He did not wake in time to go on his paper round, which meant that he had an unpleasant interview to manage when he next saw his employer. He was also late for school, and that meant that he would be in detention later in the week. He accepted this, but he found the events of the PE lesson, which preceded the history lesson, harder to bear. He had come to school without his PE kit. This was particularly unfortunate, because that had meant he was not allowed to join in the PE lesson, to which he had been looking forward as a bright spot in a rather dreary day. He had had words with the PE teacher about this and had come off the worse. His difficulties were largely due to the rather disorganised home in which he lived, but in this he was no different from many youngsters. He had put out his kit, he had cleaned his PE shoes, and all this preparation and anticipation had gone for nothing.

He had chosen history as an option in the third year, but more because of the exigencies of the school timetable than his interest in the subject. He was present at the lessons, rather than a participant in them. The lesson which marked the end of his attendance at school for the next fortnight was one in which the teacher talked to the class, and asked them to read passages from their history books. It was a rather lifeless lesson, until Martin leaned across his neighbour's desk and remarked — loudly enough for the teacher to hear, but not loudly enough for those not near them to hear — 'Who cares about the flipping Renaissance anyway?' In leaning across the desk, he knocked his history book on to the floor, but this was accidental.

The teacher, who was explaining some fact about Brunelleschi's dome, was aware that he had only a tenuous hold on the children's attention. He recognised that the lesson had not gone well and that there were other ways of presenting his material. He was really just holding on till the bell went, and was glad to notice that this would be in ten minutes' time. When Martin made his interruption, he stopped his discourse, and asked: 'What did you say?' Now he had heard what Martin had said only too well, which accounted for the challenging tone which he put into the question. He intended to convey that he was annoyed at the interruption, that he had heard what the boy had said and did not much like it. He did not intend that Martin should repeat the remark. Indeed, he meant the opposite. His question was meant to be a warning. Martin would realise that he had heard something unpleasant and, as many children do in such circumstances, he would shuffle out of the difficulty, mumbling: 'Oh, nothing, sir. I just asked Fred if he liked the Renaissance.' Unfortunately this did not happen. Martin was already sore at the morning's events, he did not particularly like history or the history teacher. The challenge in the teacher's tone further piqued him and he was ready to take him on. He was a less impressive figure than the PE teacher, whose actions in the previous lesson still smouldered in his mind. He repeated his remark, loud and clear. It produced a silence that had not hitherto been a feature of the lesson.

Whatever the teacher might have done about the first interruption, when he asked the boy what he had said, he made a mistake. He then made another. Angry at this impertinence, and conscious that he had asked for what he did not want to have, he advanced towards Martin in a series of strides, and looking angry and flustered, pointing his finger at him, he snapped: 'Pick that book up!' The confrontation was now set.

Events then followed at surprising speed. The teacher's looks, his gait and his movements further increased the challenge in the confrontation. He did not overawe Martin, but the challenge incited him to further defiance. Both he and Martin were now on the 'escalation-detonation staircase', and their subsequent challenges and responses drove each other further up it. Martin's response to the command was a surly refusal (he went up another step of the staircase). The teacher, growing increasingly angry, shouted: 'Pick it up at once!' (He went several steps higher up the stairs.) By this time, the whole class was aware that dire events were about to happen. The silence had given way to noisy interchanges that encouraged the boy and further discomforted the teacher. He was aware that the affair was slipping out of his control, and he was also conscious of the fact that the noise could be heard in the next classroom. The teacher was now standing over Martin, looking extremely angry and maintaining the tension in the confrontation by his angry presence so close to the boy.

When Martin met the command, 'Pick it up at once!' with the rejoinder, 'Pick it up yourself', another feature of the confrontation appeared — both he and the teacher began to give way to panic. Martin, for all his apparent coolness, had now defied the teacher to the point of no return, and he could not back off and disappoint the audience. At the same time, he was not sure that he could manage what he had started. He was not a hardened rebel. What was now happening was outside his experience. The teacher, conscious of the corner into which he had been manoeuvred, also gave way to panic. He made a last and unsuccessful atempt to overawe Martin, despite the evidence that this was not going to succeed. His panic prevented him from realising this and, in fact, it was his last few steps up the staircase from which the confrontation escalated. He made a verbal assault, shouting in passionate tones what he would not usually contemplate saying: 'Pick it up! Pick it up! How dare you speak to me like that? You lout! You look like a lout, you act like one! Pick that book up or I will . . . ' No one knew what the end of the sentence might have been, what threat or ultimatum was to follow. When he called Martin a lout, this so stung the boy that he got to his feet in a reflex action in the face of the assault. What then happened was confused and illustrated exactly the way in which panic leads to the misperception of intentions and actions.

Martin stood up. The teacher reached out his hand. What he meant to do, as he said afterwards, was to push the boy back into his seat. For a split second Martin saw this hand coming towards his face. He raised his hand to push it aside. In the next split second the teacher saw Martin's hand, and he thought the boy was going to strike him. He struck him with his other hand. It was not a heavy blow, but Martin returned it with a more directed punch, which knocked the teacher off balance and cut his lip. In the awful silence that followed, he ran out of the classroom. The whole confrontation, from the moment when Martin said: 'Who cares about the flipping Renaissance anyway' to his exit from the classroom, had taken just under a minute.

His flight from the classroom, the slamming of the door, following the noise of the confrontation, had brought the teacher from the next room on to the scene. He did what he could to restore order, the history teacher withdrew to the staffroom, and the lesson fizzled out. In the subsequent inquiry, Martin was suspended from school for ten days. Both he and the history teacher regretted the incident, although neither would believe the other's description of what had happened when they both raised their hands.

In analysing the origin and the development of this unpleasant incident, its antecedent events are worth considering. Although the history teacher's control of the class was not calamitous, the diminishing interest in the lesson and his lack-lustre presentation of the material had a direct bearing on the interruption which led to so much trouble. As was mentioned in Chapter 2, Redl and Wineman drew attention to the importance of injecting some stimulation into lessons, when children's attention begins to wander. The teacher did not pick up the warning signs from the class, showing that he had almost lost the initiative. When unmotivated children do not pay attention to a teacher, they very soon find something else to interest them. The teacher could have done something to renew interest in his topic. The boredom in the class was the gestation period for the crisis. Crises do not usually erupt without some warning, and we may draw an analogy from railway practice. When a fast-moving train is moving towards danger, the driver is not suddenly confronted with a red signal. The danger is indicated to him first by a double yellow signal, then a single yellow and, finally, the red one. In a class where there is trouble ahead, it is the yellow signals that alert the teacher, before the danger is upon him. In this lesson, the history teacher did not notice the yellow signals — he continued at speed to overshoot the red!

It was Martin's comment that began the series of events that led to the confrontation. The book falling on to the floor, which assumed major importance in the confrontation, was fortuitous and accidental.

As it was simultaneous with the comment the boy made, it strongly influenced the teacher's reaction. But had he had more success in dealing with what the boy said, he might have managed to keep the matter of the book in perspective.

As to the comment itself, he could hardly have ignored it. Although Martin should not have said what he did, it was not an outrageous comment. How different the outcome would have been if the teacher had said something which showed his displeasure at the interruption in more reasonable terms. Supposing he had said: 'That will do Martin. You keep your comments to yourself. Just pick up the book like a good lad and give me your attention for a few more minutes.' Or suppose he had managed a little pleasantry, saying: 'Well, Martin, Bruneschelli's dome might not be quite your cup of tea, but you wait until you see it. Now come on, it will soon be dinner time.' Or, even better: 'Martin, please stop talking to Fred. What's the matter with you anyway — you have been sitting like a bear with a sore head all morning.' This would have given the boy an opportunity to say something about his frustrating morning. He may not have taken the opportunity, but if the teacher's question was not put in a way that slighted him and if 'What's the matter with you anyway?' was said with concern and not with challenge, it is quite likely he would. Whatever the teacher said, what was needed was something which would have given him room for manoeuvre and not something which decreased this. Unless, of course, his comment was sharp enough to wrap the whole incident up at once. The fact that he said 'What did you say?' suggests that he was not able to do this — he was playing for time. He *had* heard what Martin said. Asking him 'What did you say?' was a mistake. The question might have worked out to his advantage with another child, who had not had the frustrations and disappointments that Martin had had. The teacher did not know of these, but Martin's loud repetition of what he had said took the teacher past the point when he might have given him a chance to say something, which, if it did not excuse his offence, could have been accepted as a plea in mitigation. His repetition of his comment increased the heat in the exchange, which was already beginning to show in the teacher's challenging tone. It gave the teacher less elbow room. There was now no chance of keeping the interchange following it reasonably private. Those in the class who had not heard what Martin said originally now had their attention focused on his interruption. He now had an audience.

Here the craft teacher mentioned in Chapter 7 comes into mind.

When she realised that a girl was attempting to bring on a confrontation with her, she removed her from her audience by sending her to the head of house. In the situation in the history lesson, there were two active protagonists who, between them, maintained the momentum of the confrontation, but the presence of the other children added to the momentum. Their presence and their attention, which the history teacher had aroused, influenced both him and Martin. Their involvement added to the tension, and it also made it more difficult for either Martin or the teacher to back down. Thus, the unfortunate question 'What did you say?' not only affected any following interchange between the two principals, it brought another element into the situation. It exposed it to the pressure of 24 children. More than that, the imminent drama, the tension that was now manifest, brought these 24 individuals into a more cohesive group. This reduced their chances of acting as individuals. It did not altogether prevent them, because some member of the class might have said something to Martin that would have extinguished his increasing belligerence, but it reduced the chances of this happening.

In fact, the verbal and non-verbal messages that reached both the teacher and Martin from the rest of the children illustrated some aspects of group behaviour that Cohen (1971) and Caspari (1976) explore in different ways. Cohen describes how quickly and by what means feelings and messages spread among individuals in crowds, and Caspari has interesting comments to make about roles that children play in classes. She makes the point that a bold child, or a hostile child, will act out the feelings of a class — will gather these up, so to speak, and represent them. Most of the children were bored with the lesson and the last ten minutes of it particularly. When Martin said 'Who cares about the flipping Renaissance anyway?', he said what most of them felt and would like to have said. *He* said it because he did not much care for the history teacher and because his frustrations overcame his usual restraints. These were not of a very high order anyway, and certainly not strong enough to keep back his increasing belligerence, when challenged in the ways that he was.

Before leaving this point, it is worth while to link it with one made earlier — that in some circumstances a confrontation is justifiable and may be beneficial. Before a teacher brings on a confrontation deliberately, it is important for him or her to reflect on the role of the child in the class where it comes about. If the child to be confronted *is* representing group feelings of resentment or even hostility to the teacher who brings the confrontation on, their sympathies, which might take the form of open support, will be behind the child. In the short term, when a confrontation is actually taking place, their support for a belligerent child may have important consequences. In the long term, demonstrations of support for the child, even if muted, would suggest that the teacher could look with advantage on his relationships with the class, who find their spokeschild important. This is not to suggest that a teacher should ignore a wrong because of support for the wrongdoer, but rather to emphasise the value of awareness of group behaviour. The chances of a class of children making use of one child to defy or oppose a teacher are likely to be greater, if the teacher falls into the 'deviance-provocative' category. Whereas the children in the maths classes or craft classes described in Chapter 7 would be most unlikely to signal or give support to a disruptive child, they would do it with a will in the geography lesson.

Returning to the confrontation in the history lesson, it can be seen that after Martin had repeated the remark about the Renaissance, the teacher had lost the initiative. He tried to regain it, but his attempt not only failed, it made matters worse. There was clear evidence that Martin was not going to be overawed. If he had, he would not have repeated his comment with such sang-froid. Anyone not as wound up as the teacher was could see that the boy was intent on a power struggle, and that he would match whatever the teacher would contribute to it. Thus, the angry advance, the strides, the pointed finger emphasised the teacher's challenge and prompted Martin to increase his. The situation could probably have been saved, if, instead of switching attention to the fallen book, the teacher had concentrated on Martin's comment. It would have been better *had he stood where he was,* and done his best to recover from the error he made in asking for the repetition. It was when he advanced so challengingly that both he and Martin began to ascend the escalation-detonation staircase.

Angry teachers sometimes forget how much of a challenge they present to children when they advance towards them. If this overawes a child, then further difficulties do not follow. But if it serves only to provoke a counter-challenge and exacerbate the situation, it is plainly counter-productive. Whereas teachers recognise that what they say can bring on hostile reactions, they tend to be less aware of the effects of their facial expressions, their gait and gestures as these demonstrate their anger or impatience. Non-verbal communications can be very explicit; body language can be very strong language. Certainly the history teacher was unaware of what his gait, his raised arm and outraged expression were doing to Martin. At the same time, he was unaware of the effect on him of his increasing proximity.

It was when the teacher shouted 'Pick it up at once!' that the panic began to influence the confrontation. Neither of them could now easily back down, but one of them could have done something, or said something, which would have interrupted the swift ascent up the staircase. Unless one of them did this, it was almost certain that they would reach the point of detonation − the top of the staircase. As Martin showed it was not going to be him, it was up to the senior partner to back off. He was, after all, the more mature of the two. The situation was deplorable, but as it had reached the stage it had, all that was left was for the teacher to save what he could. He could have saved his dignity at least.

Backing off is not a pleasant prospect for a teacher, but it has to be weighed against the alternative. As he and Martin were now eyeball to eyeball, any further provocation was bound to lead to some physical encounter, as the children in the class realised − they were waiting for it to happen. In such a physical struggle, especially as there was no clear physical advantage on either side, the outcome was unpredictable. It is better for a teacher, in such circumstances, to avoid this than to attempt it and to be worsted in it. Even if it is successful, it is undignified and demeaning. Whatever else an audience of children may say about a teacher's behaviour, if he backs off before the physical encounter begins, they will at least recognise that he has preserved some of his adult status by refusing to be drawn into physical combat. Unhappily, the history teacher's anger and the panic in the situation so clouded his judgement that he did not even wait for a response to his command. He followed it immediately by the verbal assault that marked the detonation at the top of the staircase. From that moment on, the situation was lost.

It began with a provocative and uncalled for comment and an accident. Within sixty seconds, it ended in a disaster which neither of the principals foresaw and neither wished. The outcome was out of all proportion to the original offence. Martin should not have said what he did or have done what he did. But at no time did the teacher allow an opportunity for the momentum of the confrontation to subside. He was caught up in the tension that he, as well as the boy, maintained in the confrontation. There were opportunities on each step of the staircase for one of them to call a halt. As the older, more responsible partner, the teacher should have pocketed his pride and taken that initiative. It was not a pleasant thing to have to do, but what happened was worse. It was true that, as Martin was suspended, he did not 'get away with it'.

But no one gave the teacher credit for the affair — it was not as if he had made an example of a hardened and persistent offender. The history teacher himself regretted what happened.

The description of the confrontation between Martin and the history teacher shows how rapidly such a situation may deteriorate once a teacher makes an initial error in the management of an unexpected disruptive incident. Initial errors are often compounded when confused thinking, anxiety, anger and panic combine to accelerate the decline towards unpredictable and regrettable outcomes. There are many classroom situations where teachers have much to bear. They are vulnerable, as all individuals are, but because they have to meet stresses and challenges that are peculiar to their profession, their vulnerabilities are likely to be exposed. In some situations, although such exposure is unpleasant, this does not lead to serious consequences. In others it plainly does. In this book, we have shown how teachers can avoid the errors that the history teacher made. The effects on the class of his unsuccessful confrontation, its effects on his subsequent management of his classes and the consequences for Martin could have been avoided had he been more aware of appropriate techniques of classroom management.

REFERENCES

Becker, W.C., Engelmann, S. and Thomas, D.R. (1975) *Teaching 1: Classroom Management*, SRA, Chicago

Becker, W.C. Madsen, C.H. Arnold, C.R. and Thomas, D.R. (1967) 'The Contingent Use of Teacher Attention and Priase in Reducing Classroom Behaviour Problems', *Journal of Special Education*, vol. 1, no. 3, pp. 287-307

Brophy, J.E. (1979) 'Advances in Teacher Effectiveness Research' in H.F.Clarizio, R.C. Craig and W.A. Mehrens *Contemporary Issues in Educational Psychology*, 4th edn, Allyn and Bacon, Boston

Brophy, J.E. and Evertson, C.M. (1976) *Learning from Teaching: A Developmental Perspective*, Allyn and Bacon, Boston

Brophy, J.E. and Good, T.L. (1974) *Teacher-Student Relationship: Causes and Consequences*, Holt, Rinehart and Winston, New York

Bruner, J. (1966) *Towards a Theory of Instruction*, Harvard University Press, Cambridge, Massachusetts

Buckley, N.U. and Walker, H.M. (1970) *Modifying Classroom Behaviour*, Research Press, Champaign, Illinois

Carter, R. (1972) *Help! These Kids are Driving Me Crazy*, Research Press, Champaign, Illinois

Caspari, I.E. (1976) *Troublesome Children in Class*, Routledge and Kegan Paul, London

Charles, C.M. and Malian, I.M. (1980) *The Special Student: Practical Help for the Classroom Teacher*, Mosby, St Louis

Chazan, M., Laing, A., Bailey, M.S. and Jones, E. (1981) 'Young Children with Special Needs in the Ordinary School' in W. Swann (ed.), *The Practice of Special Education*, Open University Milton Keynes, and Basil Blackwell, Oxford

Chester, J. and Avis, P. (1977) *Make It Count: Puzzles*, National Extension College, Cambridge

Clarizio, H.F. (1976) *Towards Positive Classroom Behaviour*, Wiley, New York

Cohen, A.K. (1971) *Delinquent Boys: The Culture of the Gang*, Collier Macmillan, London

Dohrenwend, B.P. (1961) 'The Psychological Nature of Stress', *Journal of Abnormal Psychology*, vol. 62, no. 2, pp. 294-302

Dreikurs, R. (1968) *Psychology in the Classroom*, Harper and Row, New York

Dreikurs, R., Grunwald, B.B. and Pepper, F.C. (1971) *Maintaining Sanity in the Classroom*, Harper and Row, New York

Dunham, J. (1976) 'Stress Situations and Responses' in *Stress in Schools*, National Association of Schoolmasters and National Union of Women Teachers, London

Egan, M.W. (1981) 'Strategies for Behavioural Programming' in M.L. Hardman, M.W. Egan and E.D. London (eds), *What Will We Do in the Morning?*, W.L. Brown, Dubuque, Iowa

Epps, P. and Deans, J. (1972) *Mathematical Games*, Macmillan, London

Evertson, C.M. (1982) 'Differences in Instructional Activities in Higher and Lower Achieving Junior High English and Maths Classes', *Elementary School Journal*, vol. 82, pp. 329-50

Francis, P. (1975) *Beyond Control?* Allen and Unwin, London

Galwey, J. (1970) 'Classroom Discipline', *Comprehensive Education*, vol. 4, pp. 24-6

Gardner, K. (1980) 'Failure to Read: Not Reading Failure' in M.Clark and E.Glynn *Reading and Writing for the Child with Difficulties*, Birmingham University

Gnagey, W.J. (1981) *Motivating Classroom Discipline*, Macmillan, New York

Good, T.L. and Brophy, J.E. (1980) *Educational Psychology: A Realistic Approach*, Holt, Rinehart and Winston, New York

Hallahan, D.P. and Kauffman, J.M. (1978) *Exceptional Children: An Introduction to Special Education*, Prentice Hall, Englewood Cliffs, New Jersey

Hargreaves, D.H., Hestor, S.K., Mellor, F.J. (1975) *Deviance in Classrooms*, Routledge and Kegan Paul, London

Harré, R. and Rosser, E. (1975) 'The Rules of Disorder', *Times Educational Supplement* (25 July 1975)

Harrison, C. (1980) *Readability in the Classroom*, Cambridge University Press, Cambridge

Hawisher, M.F. and Calhoun, M.L. (1978) *The Resource Room: An Educational Asset for Children with Special Needs*, Merrill, Columbus, Ohio

Hebb, D.O. (1972) *Textbook of Psychology*, Saunders, Eastbourne

Hegarty, S., Pocklington, K. Lucas, D. (1982) *Integration in Action*, National Foundation for Educational Research, Nelson, Walton-on-Thames

Henson, K.T. and Higgins, J.E. (1978) *Personalizing Teaching in the Elementary School*, Merrill, Columbus, Ohio

Herbert, M. (1978) *Conduct Disorders of Childhood and Adolescence*, Wiley, Chichester

Heron, T.E. (1978) 'Maintaining the Mainstreamed Child in the Regular Classroom: the Decision Making Process', *Journal of Learning Disabilities*, vol. 11, no. 4, pp. 26-32

Homme, L. (1970) *How To Use Contingency Contracting in the Classroom*, Research Press, Champaign, Illinois

Hopkins, B.L. and Conard, R.J. (1976) 'Putting It All Together: Super School' in Haring, N.G. and Schiefelbush, R.C. *Teaching Special Children*, McGraw Hill, New York

House, E.R. and Lapan, S.D. (1978) *Survival in the Classroom: Negotiating with Kids, Colleagues and Bosses*, Allyn and Bacon, Boston

Johnson, D.W. and Johnson, R.T. (1975) *Teaching Together and Alone: Co-operation, Competition and Individualisation*, Prentice-Hall, Englewood Cliffs, New Jersey

Jones, V.F. and Jones, L.S. (1981) *Responsible Classroom Discipline*, Allyn and Bacon, Boston

Jordan, J. (1974) 'The Organisation of Perspectives in Teacher-Pupil Relations: An Interactionist Approach', Unpublished MEd Thesis, University of Manchester

Kounin, J.S. (1970) *Discipline and Group Management in Classrooms*, Holt, Rinehart and Winston, New York

Kyriacou, C. (1980) 'High Anxiety', *Times Educational Supplement* (6 June 1980)

Kyriacou, C. and Sutcliffe, J. (1977) 'Teacher Stress: A Review', *Educational Review*, vol. 29, no. 4, pp. 299-304

Laslett, R. (1977) *Educating Maladjusted Children*, Staples, Crosby Lockwood, London

Laslett, R. (1982) *Maladjusted Children in the Ordinary School*, National Council for Special Education, Stratford-upon-Avon

Leach, D.J. and Raybould, E.C. (1977) *Learning and Behaviour Difficulties in School*, Open Books, London

Lemlech, J.K. (1979) *Classroom Management*, Harper and Row, New York

Lindgen, J.A. (1960) 'Neuroses of School Teachers: A Colloquy, *Mental Hygiene*, vol. 44, pp. 79-90

Long, N.J. and Newman, R.G. (1976) 'Managing Surface Behaviour of Children in School' in N.J. Long, W.C. Morse and R.G. Newman, *Conflict in the Class-room*, 3rd edn, Wadsworth, Belmont, California

Lovitt, T.C. (1977) *In Spite of My Resistance: I've Learned from Children*, Merrill, Columbus, Ohio

Lunzer, E. and Gardner, K. (1979) *The Effective Use of Reading*, Heinemann, London

McNicholas, J. and McEntee, J. (1973) *Games to Develop Reading Skills*, National Association for Remedial Education, Stafford

Marland, M. (1975) *The Craft of the Classroom: A Survival Guide*, Heinemann, London

Marsh, G.E. and Price, B.J. (1980) *Methods for Teaching the Mildly Handicapped Adolescent*, Mosby, St Louis

Martin, R.J. (1980) *Teaching through Encouragement: Techniques to Help Students Learn*, Prentice-Hall, Englewood Cliffs, New Jersey

Martin, R. and Lauridsen, D. (1974) *Developing Student Discipline and Motivation*, Research Press, Champaign, Illinois

Meighan, R.M. (1978) *A Sociology of Educating*, Holt, Rinehart and Winston, London

Mills, W.C.P. (1976) 'The Seriously Disruptive Behaviour of Pupils in Secondary Schools of one Local Authority', unpublished MEd thesis, Birmingham University

Neisworth, J.T. and Smith, R.M. (1973) *Modifying Retarded Behaviour*, Houghton Mifflin, Boston

O'Leary, K.D. and O'Leary, S.E. (1977) *Classroom Management*, Pergamon Press, New York

Pik, R. (1981) 'Confrontation Situations and Teacher Support Systems' in B. Gillham (ed.), *Problem Behaviour in the Secondary School*, Croom Helm, London

Poteet, J.A. (1973) *Behaviour Modification: A Practical Guide for Teachers*, University of London Press, London

Redl, F. (1971) 'The Concept of Punishment' in N.J. Long, W.C. Morse and R.G. Newman (eds.), *Conflict in the Classroom*, 3rd edn, Wadsworth, Belmont, California

Redl, F. and Wineman, D. (1951) *Children Who Hate*, Free Press, New York

Redl, F. and Wineman, D. (1952) *Controls from Within*, Free Press, New York

Roberts, B. (1977) 'Treating Children in Secondary Schools', *Educational Review*, vol. 29, no. 3, pp. 204-12

Robertson, J. (1981) *Effective Classroom Control*, Hodder and Stoughton, London

Roe, A.M. (1978) 'Medical and Psychological Concepts of Problem Behaviour', in B. Gillham, *Reconstructing Educational Psychology*, Croom Helm, London

Rosenthal, R. and Jacobson, L.F. (1968) *Pygmalion in the Classroom*, Holt, Rinehart and Winston, New York

Rutter, M. and Madge, N. (1977) *Cycles of Disadvantage*, Heinemann, London

Rutter, M., Tizard, J. and Whitmore, K. (1970) *Education, Health and Behaviour*, Longman, London

Rutter, M., Maughan, B., Mortimore, P. and Ouston, J. (1979) *Fifteen Thousand Hours: Secondary Schools and their Effects on Children*, Open Books, London

Saunders, M. (1979) *Class Control and Behaviour*, McGraw Hill, London

Sewell, G. (1982) *Reshaping Remedial Education*, Croom Helm, London

Skinner, B.F. (1968) *The Technology of Teaching*, Appleton-Century Crofts, New York

Sloane, H.N. (1976) *Classroom Management: Remediation and Prevention*, Wiley, New York

Smith, C.J. (1982) 'Helping Colleagues Cope: A Consultant Role for the Remedial Teacher', *Remedial Education* vol. 17, no. 2, pp. 75-8

Smith, S.L. (1979) *No Easy Answers: Teaching the Learning Disabled Child*, Winthrop, Cambridge, Massachusetts

Stott, D.H. (1978) *Helping Children with Learning Difficulties*, Ward Lock Educational, London

Tanner, L.N. (1978) *Classroom Discipline*, Holt, Rinehart and Winston, New York

Ullman, L. and Krasner, L. (1965) *Case Studies in Behaviour Modification*, Holt, Rinehart and Winston, New York

Vargas, J.S. (1977) *Behavioural Psychology for Teachers*, Harper and Row, New York

Wallace, G. and Kauffman, J.M. (1978) *Teaching Children with Learning Problems*, Merrill, Columbus, Ohio

Weber, K.J. (1982) *The Teacher is the Key: A Practical Guide for Teaching the Adolescent with Learning Difficulties*, Open University Press, Milton Keynes

Wilson, M. and Evans, M. (1980) *Education of Disturbed Pupils*, Methuen, London

Wragg, E.C. (1978) 'Death by a Thousand Workcards?' *Times Educational Supplement* (3 November 1978)

SUBJECT INDEX

AUTHOR INDEX